HARVARD THEOLOGICAL STUDIES
I

# THE COMPOSITION AND DATE OF ACTS

BY

CHARLES CUTLER TORREY

PROFESSOR OF THE SEMITIC LANGUAGES
IN YALE UNIVERSITY

PUBLISHERS
*Eugene, Oregon*

Wipf and Stock Publishers
199 W 8th Ave, Suite 3
Eugene, OR 97401

The Composition and Date of Acts
By Torrey, Charles C.
ISBN: 1-59752-159-0
Publication date 4/25/2005
Previously published by Harvard University Press, 1916

# THE COMPOSITION AND DATE OF ACTS

## CHAPTER I

### THE ARAMAIC SOURCE IN ACTS 1-15

#### § 1. INTRODUCTORY

THE hypothesis of a Semitic source (or sources) underlying more or less of the first half of Acts has commended itself to a few scholars. Thus Harnack, *Lukas der Arzt*, 1906, p. 84: " Es spricht Wichtiges dafür, dass Lukas in der ersten Hälfte der Acta eine aramäische Quelle übersetzt und benutzt hat, aber schlagend kann die Annahme nicht widerlegt werden, dass er lediglich auf mündlichen Mitteilungen fusst. Vollends unsicher ist es, welchen Umfang die Quelle gehabt hat und ob es überhaupt eine einzige Quelle gewesen ist." Similarly in his *Apostelgeschichte*, 1908, pp. 138, 186. Wendt, *Die Apostelgeschichte*, 1913, p. 16, says: " Im Anschluss an Nestle *StKr* 1896 S. 102 ff. nimmt [Blass] die Bearbeitung einer aramäischen Quelle im ersten Teile der Apostelgeschichte an. Die in diesem ersten Teile häufiger als im zweiten vorliegenden Aramaismen werden von ihm als Beweis hierfür betrachtet (*Evang. sec. Luc.*, 1897, p. vi, xxi, ss.)." See also Blass' very meager statement in his *Philology of the Gospels* (1898), 141, 193 f., 201, of his somewhat hastily conceived theory according to which Luke followed an Aramaic source in the first *twelve* chapters of Acts.

But so far as I am aware, no one has ever attempted to point out specifically Aramaic locutions in Acts. Nor has the search for Semitisms, of whatever sort, hitherto resulted in any fruitful discovery. A few doubtful examples have been adduced in support of still more doubtful conclusions; there has been no effort to collect and examine the material of this nature. Nestle's observations, referred to above,[1] were concerned only with two variant readings (2, 47 and 3, 14) in Codex Bezae, and have no bearing whatever on the question of the original language of this part of Acts, as I hope to have opportunity to show elsewhere.[2] Wellhausen in his " Noten zur Apostelgeschichte " (*Nachrichten von der K. Gesellsch. der Wiss. zu Göttingen*, 1907, 1-21) takes no notice of Semitisms or of possible Semitic sources; in his " Kritische Analyse der Apostelgeschichte " (*Abhandlungen der K. Gesellsch. der Wiss. zu Göttingen*, 1914, 1-56) he considers the possibility of translation in only one passage, namely 2, 23 f., and there in a wholly non-committal way. Among English and American scholars the question of Semitic sources in Acts seems to have aroused even less interest than among the Germans. Moffatt, *Introduction*, 1911, p. 290, says (citing Harnack): " There is fair ground for conjecturing that Luke used and translated an Aramaic source "; and Milligan, *The New Testament Documents*, 1913, p. 163, refers to the hypothesis as a possible one.

Now Aramaic is not an unknown language, and we have considerable familiarity with the principles and methods of those who rendered Semitic documents into Greek at the beginning of the present era. The question, too, is one of far-reaching importance. In a writing of the character and extent of the first half of Acts it would ordinarily be possible to determine whether the Greek is a translation, and if so, from what language the version was made. In the present case, by good fortune, the material at hand for the demonstration is more than usually satisfactory. I am confident that those who examine the evidence carefully will find it conclusive.

## § 2. The Language of the First Half of Acts

The first half of the Book of Acts is concerned primarily with the church in Jerusalem, viewed as the center from which great evangelizing forces went out into the world. The background of the narra-

---

[1] They were first published in English in *The Expositor*, 1895, pp. 235-239; then, with the title " Einige Beobachtungen zum Codex Bezä," in the *Theol. Studien u. Kritiken*, l. c.

[2] It should be added that Nestle's own conclusion as to the original language indicated was that it was more likely Hebrew than Aramaic (*Expositor, l. c.*, p. 238); see however his *Philologica Sacra*, 1896, p. 55, where he refuses to express an opinion.

tive is obviously Judean. It is antecedently probable that the earliest documents of this Jewish-Christian community would have been written in Aramaic, the vernacular. We also have excellent reason for believing that Luke,[1] the compiler of the two histories, was one who made special search for Semitic documents, as the primitive and authentic sources, in order to render them into Greek. I think I may claim, without undue presumption, that the whole question of Semitic sources in Acts has entered a new phase since my argument, in the article "The Translations made from the Original Aramaic Gospels," contributed to *Studies in the History of Religions Presented to Crawford Howell Toy* (New York, Macmillan Co., 1912, pp. 269-317), that the compiler of the Third Gospel was an accomplished translator of both Hebrew and Aramaic.[2] We should therefore surmise, at the outset, that the very noticeable Semitic coloring of the first part of the book, remarked by all commentators, is simply due to translation.

It is not necessary to argue that the Greek of Acts is not homogeneous; it may be well, however, to review here the main facts touching the question of translation. For the first fifteen chapters, the language is distinctly translation-Greek; in the remaining chapters, on the contrary, the idiom is not Semitic, and there is no evidence that we are dealing with a version. The whole book, however, shows unmistakable uniformity of vocabulary and phraseology, so that it is obvious (to him who recognizes the Semitic source) that the author of 16-28 was the translator of 1-15. Many have remarked that the most strongly "Hebraizing" chapters are those at the beginning of the book. The reason for this appearance is the fact that the opening chapters are so largely made up of speeches composed in high style, along with quotations from the Old Testa-

[1] The identification of the author of the Third Gospel and Acts with Luke, the companion of Paul, is not essential to the present argument. I will, however, record here my opinion that the church tradition is right, and that Luke the compiler was also the author of the "We-document."

[2] The article was not reviewed or noticed in print, so far as I am aware, but the many letters which I received lead me to think that the demonstration was generally accepted by those who read it. Most of the letters expressly approved the argument derived from Luke 1, 39, in particular, and no one of my correspondents raised objection to it.

ment. The case is exactly parallel to that of the first two chapters of Luke's Gospel. On the other hand, in such chapters as Acts 13–15, where the events narrated are comparatively recent and widely familiar, and the language therefore is that of every-day life, the rendering sounds somewhat more free. But even in the chapters of this latter class the translation is found on examination to be truly close; the Greek idiom never strays far from the Aramaic, while occasional telltale phrases point to the underlying language. These indications of a translated Semitic source, it may be added, are present in every part of the first half of the book. There are no passages in which the *language* can be said to make it probable that Luke is composing his own Greek. It is a striking fact (which will be considered more fully below) that in the very beginning of the first chapter the evidence from the material content combines with that afforded by the language in such a way as to make it plain that Luke is following a written source so closely, and with such self-restraint, that he does not even allow himself space for an introductory sentence of his own. This, again, is altogether characteristic of the author of the Third Gospel.

Throughout chapters 1–15 we are constantly meeting such Semitisms as the following:[1] 1, 1 ἤρξατο ποιεῖν (Aram.); 1, 5 μετὰ πολλὰς ταύτας ἡμέρας (Jewish Aram.); 1, 10 καὶ ὡς (וּכְדִי) ἀτενίζοντες ἦσαν . . . καὶ ἰδού (וַהֲא) κ.τ.λ.; 1, 15 ἐπὶ τὸ αὐτό (also 2, 1, 44, 47); 2, 7 οὐχὶ ἰδού (Aram.); 2, 23 ἔκδοτον διὰ χειρὸς (בְּיַד) ἀνόμων;[2] 3, 20 καιροὶ ἀναψύξεως ἀπὸ προσώπου τοῦ κυρίου; 4, 12 τὸ δεδομένον ἐν ἀνθρώποις; 4, 16 γνωστὸν σημεῖον (Aram.); 4, 30 ἐν τῷ τὴν χεῖρα ἐκτείνειν σε; 5, 4 τί ὅτι ἔθου ἐν τῇ καρδίᾳ σου; 5, 28 παραγγελίᾳ παρηγγείλαμεν; 5, 41 ἀπὸ προσώπου τοῦ συνεδρίου; 6, 5 καὶ ἤρεσεν ὁ λόγος ἐνώπιον παντὸς τοῦ πλήθους; 7, 13 ἐν τῷ δευτέρῳ

---

[1] I give here only a selection; it would be easy to make the list much longer. I have designated those idioms which are specifically Aramaic; those which are not thus designated might be either Aramaic or Hebrew. The Aramaic equivalents not given here will be found in the sequel. Some of these idioms are to be found occasionally in the Koiné, but no specimen of the Koiné ever showed such an array as this!

[2] Cf. Wellhausen, *Kritische Analyse*, 5 (this is the passage in which he touches the question of a Semitic source). In the original Aramaic the words were the same as those in Mark 14, 41, and the rendering should have been εἰς χεῖρας.

ἐγνωρίσθη τοῖς ἀδελφοῖς αὐτοῦ; 7, 23 ἀνέβη ἐπὶ τὴν καρδίαν αὐτοῦ (Aram.); 7, 53 εἰς διαταγὰς ἀγγέλων; 8, 6 ἐν τῷ ἀκούειν αὐτούς; 9, 3 ἐν δὲ τῷ πορεύεσθαι ἐγένετο αὐτὸν ἐγγίζειν; 9, 22 ἐνεδυναμοῦτο (Aram., אתחיל); 9, 32 διὰ πάντων; 10, 14 οὐδέποτε (לָא מִיוֹמַי) ἔφαγον πᾶν (כֹל) κοινόν; 10, 15 πάλιν ἐκ δευτέρου (probably עוֹד תִּנְיָנוּת; so also Matt. 26, 42); 10, 25 ἐγένετο τοῦ εἰσελθεῖν; 11, 4 ἀρξάμενος (Aram.); 11, 22 ἠκούσθη εἰς τὰ ὦτα; 12, 3 προσέθετο συλλαβεῖν; 12, 10 προῆλθον ῥύμην μίαν (חד for indefinite article; even more common in Aramaic than in Hebrew); 13, 11 καὶ νῦν ἰδοὺ χεὶρ Κυρίου ἐπὶ σέ; and also ἄχρι καιροῦ (עַד עִדָּן, Dan. 7, 12 etc.); 13, 12 ἐκπληττόμενος ἐπὶ (עַל) τῇ διδαχῇ; 13, 24 πρὸ προσώπου τῆς εἰσόδου αὐτοῦ; 13, 25 οὐκ εἰμὶ ἐγώ (Aram.); 14, 2 ἐκάκωσαν τὰς ψυχὰς τῶν ἐθνῶν; 14, 8 χωλὸς ἐκ κοιλίας μητρὸς αὐτοῦ (also 3, 2); 14, 15 εὐαγγελιζόμενοι ὑμᾶς ἐπιστρέφειν ἐπὶ θεὸν ζῶντα; 15, 4 παρεδέχθησαν ἀπὸ τῆς ἐκκλησίας (אתקבל מן, the invariable idiom in Aramaic. Correction to ὑπό, as in most MSS., was inevitable); 15, 7 ἐν ὑμῖν ἐξελέξατο (see below); 15, 3 ἀπεκρίθη Ἰάκωβος (the very common Aramaic ענה "take up the word," sometimes hardly more than "speak"; cf. Dan. 4, 27! So also 3, 12 and 5, 8);[1] 15, 23 οἱ πρεσβύτεροι ἀδελφοί.

The fact that so many of these idioms are obviously Aramaic, while no specifically (or even prevailingly) Hebrew idiom is to be found, is certainly not accidental. Moreover, it is not enough to speak of frequent Semitisms; the truth is that the language of all these fifteen chapters is translation-Greek through and through, generally preserving even the order of words.

In the remainder of the book, chapters 16–28, the case is altogether different. Here, there is no evidence of an underlying Semitic language. The few apparent Semitisms (καὶ ἰδού; ἐγένετο with infin.; τότε used in continuing a narrative; ἐνώπιον with gen.; ἔθετο ἐν τῷ πνεύματι πορεύεσθαι; ἐκ μέσου (ἐν μέσῳ) αὐτῶν) are chargeable to the Koiné; though their presence may be due in part to the influence of the translation-Greek which Luke had so exten-

---

[1] The idiom is also Hebrew. As for 2 Macc. 15, 14, it was written by a man who, as we have good reason to believe, was as familiar with Aramaic as with Greek (see my *Aramaic Gospels*, 295).

sively read and written. In either case they are negligible. Luke's own language — if that is really what we have in the latter half of Acts — has a simplicity of structure that is often much like the Semitic, and this fact renders the transition less abrupt. Harnack, *Apostelgeschichte* 16, says: " Im allgemeinen kommt Lukas' Stil dem der Septuaginta, namentlich aber dem der Makkabäerbücher (der aber selbst nichts anderes ist als der Stil der gesprochenen Sprache, von gebildeten Männern behandelt) sehr nahe." Whoever is well acquainted with the literature here named will rub his eyes when he reads these words. The " style " of the LXX is simply the style of literal translations from Semitic originals, the clumsy result of putting Hebrew writings into a too closely fitting Greek dress. Luke's style in Acts 16–28 (the only place, excepting Luke 1, 1–4, where we can really examine it) has in it scarcely anything to remind us of the Greek Old Testament. In structure, syntax, and idioms habitually employed its Greek belongs to an altogether different genus. And what is "the style of the Books of Maccabees"? 1 Macc. is a closely literal rendering from a Hebrew original. The style of 2 Macc. is rhetorical, somewhat labored, and much more pretentious than that of Luke, and is totally different from that of 1 Macc. The style of 3 Macc. is so overloaded and bombastic as to make the book very tiresome reading. In 4 Macc. we have the work of a master of Alexandrian rhetoric, but his style has hardly any resemblance to that of Luke. The Greek of Acts 16–28, then, is *not* " like that of the LXX," to say nothing of the widely diverse Books of Maccabees. Furthermore, even if we substitute "language" for " style," it is not true that Acts 1–15 sounds like the Koiné. It sounds, on the contrary, like 1 Macc., Jeremiah, Daniel, and all the other translations from Hebrew or Aramaic. The voice of the Aramaic can be heard through the Greek. Luke translates like the best interpreters of his time, always faithfully and generally word for word. When he writes his own language, on the other hand, the resulting Greek represents a Syrian type of the Koiné which reads smoothly and is sufficiently idiomatic.[1] In short, the Greek of the

[1] In some respects the Greek of Marcus Diaconus' *Life of Porphyrius of Gaza* offers an interesting parallel to that of Acts 16–28, after due allowance has been made for the

first half of Acts differs widely and constantly from that of the second half, both in the idiom which it uses and in its literary structure. There is one obvious and satisfactory way of accounting for this fact, namely the hypothesis of translation in the first half. Is there any other adequate explanation?[1]

It is perhaps unnecessary to say that any attempt to reconstruct the Judean Aramaic dialect of the middle of the first century is bound to be arbitrary, and that the result can only be an artificial idiom. We must rely chiefly on our meager knowledge of the Aramaic of the " Biblical " period (3d–2d centuries B.C.), and our hardly more satisfactory acquaintance with the dialect of the Onkelos Targum (mainly second century A.D.; a translation idiom, with all the usual characteristics of such a creation). We have also the valuable, though very scanty, aid afforded by the *Megillath Taanith* and other bits of the genuine Judean speech of the first or second century which have been preserved in the Talmud and elsewhere. The many other helps, necessary but of minor importance, need not be mentioned here. Questions as to the type of speech most likely to be employed in such a narrative as this in Acts, whether popular or formal, whether archaizing or representing actually current use, are perhaps a mere waste of time. The answer to them, moreover, would not in the least affect the results reached in any of the passages discussed in the following pages. In my own attempts at retranslation I have been guided by the probability that since this is distinctly a literary composition, and also written from the standpoint of the Jewish sacred tradition, its diction may well be supposed to have inclined toward that of the older models. At all events, the words and phrases here conjectured are all truly Aramaic and Palestinian, and possible of use at the time supposed.

interval of time between the two writings. The style is very simple, and the language contains some distinct Syriasms (just as Luke's frequent use of τότε, " thereupon," is probably due to the influence of the Aramaic אדין). Luke's style, however, is even more direct and effective, and also stands on a higher literary plane.

[1] In regard to the untenability of the theory that Luke " imitated the LXX " I have expressed myself at some length elsewhere (*Aramaic Gospels*, pp. 285–288).

§ 3. Especially Striking Examples of Mistranslation
in Acts 1-15

Especially striking evidence of translation in chapters 1-15 is afforded by the following passages. I have put first a number of examples of serious mistranslation; then follows a collection of minor slips, including too literal renderings. This latter list could be considerably lengthened.

**2, 47.** The most interesting of all the phrases which suggest translation is found in 2, 47. The narrator is telling how the first large body of believers was formed in Jerusalem, as the result of those things which happened on the day of Pentecost. The new community was harmonious within, and was looked upon with favor by all the people of the city: "Day by day, continuing steadfastly with one accord in the temple, and breaking bread at home, they did take their food with gladness and singleness of heart, praising God and having favor with all the people." Verse 47 then continues: ὁ δὲ κύριος προσετίθει τοὺς σωζομένους καθ' ἡμέραν ἐπὶ τὸ αὐτό. Excepting the last three words, this is just what we should expect: a general statement regarding the increase of the newly formed church, similar to the statements made at frequent intervals (4, 4; 5, 14; 6, 7; 9, 31, etc.), throughout this narrative. But the words ἐπὶ τὸ αὐτό have remained an unsolved riddle. The phrase ordinarily means "together," "in the same place"; in the Greek Old Testament it is the standing equivalent of יַחַד and יַחְדָּו. It has just been used in this chapter, vs. 44: "And all that believed were *together*, and had all things common." Other passages in Luke—Acts are: Luke 17, 35, "Two women shall be grinding *together*"; Acts 1, 15, "A multitude of persons *together*"; 2, 1, "They were all *together* in one place." Cf. also 4, 26, where the phrase is taken over from the Greek Old Testament (Ps. 2, 2 ἐπὶ τὸ αὐτό = יַחַד). But in 2, 47, the passage under discussion, the meaning "together" is obviously inadmissible. It is true that Lumby in the Cambridge Bible, with the scholar's wish to follow well-known usage, renders: "And the Lord added day by day together such as were in the way of salvation"; but other scholars will see in this only a bit of "translation-English," a rendering of the kind so familiar in the Greek Bible — and possibly exemplified in this very ἐπὶ τὸ αὐτό as it stands before us so ill-suited to its context.

The ancient interpreters felt the difficulty of the phrase, and tried in various ways to overcome it. In the *textus receptus* the attempt is made to join the troublesome words to the following verse, making them the beginning of 3, 1: " Now *together* Peter and John went up to the temple," etc.; a futile expedient which, however, bears eloquent witness to the inability of early readers — who really knew Greek — to give the ἐπὶ τὸ αὐτό any plausible connection with the preceding context. Many old manuscripts and versions endeavor to improve the passage by inserting τῇ ἐκκλησίᾳ (a dative is to be expected after προσετίθει) or ἐν τῇ ἐκκλησίᾳ, either before or after the three words under discussion, in order to remove as much of the obscurity as possible. Thus, for example, Cod. D has . . . καθ' ἡμέραν ἐπὶ τὸ αὐτὸ ἐν τῇ ἐκκλησίᾳ. This form of the insertion might seem to provide a foothold for the ἐπὶ τὸ αὐτό, and it is therefore worthy of especial notice that the Syriac version and its congeners connect the latter phrase with 3, 1, although reading ἐν τῇ ἐκκλησίᾳ.[1]

Modern commentators and interpreters have passed around the difficulty in more or less unhappy fashion. The Revisers of 1881 render: " And the Lord added *to them* day by day those that were being saved," but remark in the margin that instead of " *to them* " the Greek reads " *together* "; that is, they really do not render the phrase at all. In Weizsäcker's N.T. we read: " Der Herr aber fügte *ihrer Vereinigung* täglich bei, die sich retten liessen "; but the Greek cannot possibly mean this. Preuschen (in Lietzmann's *Handbuch*; 1912) omits the phrase in his translation, remarking: " ἐπὶ τὸ αὐτό verstärkt hier lediglich die Präposition in προσετίθει." So far as this is an explanation at all, it means that either Preuschen or the author of Acts cared nothing for Greek usage. Wendt (in Meyer's *Komm.*; 1913) renders: " zu dem Zusammensein," but

---

[1] The testimony of the Peshitta here has been commonly misunderstood and misstated; thus in Von Soden's *Schriften des N. T.* it is given incorrectly in both verses. The word *akhedā* (= יחד) in 3, 1 is unquestionably the rendering of ἐπὶ τὸ αὐτό.

straightway replaces this by a different rendering: " auf denselben Ort hin," formerly adopted by Holtzmann (*Handcomm.*), who however recognized its great difficulty. This last suggestion in fact does justice neither to Greek usage nor to the historical situation. The incipient church in Jerusalem was not confined to any one meeting place in such a way that the narrator could have said: " The Lord daily added new converts (and brought them) *to the same place* " ; nor, if he had wished to say this, would he have employed words which seem to mean something else. The early Church Fathers and scribes of the sacred text could not be satisfied with any of these attempts at explanation; they saw clearly that something was wrong with the Greek as it was first handed down to them. We also may say with confidence either that the Greek of 2, 47, in the oldest form known to us, has suffered corruption, or else that its author was writing under some such compulsion as that of translation.

Under these circumstances, the hypothesis of translation from a Semitic original certainly deserves to be considered. When the test of retroversion into Aramaic is applied, the result is unexpectedly interesting, for it not only provides an easy solution of the difficulty of the passage, but also seems to furnish direct evidence that author and translator lived in different parts of the Aramaic-speaking world.

Of the possible Aramaic equivalents of the Greek ἐπὶ τὸ αὐτό, Hebrew יַחְדָּו, only one needs to be considered, namely the adverbial compound לַחֲדָא, לְחֲדָא. Etymologically, this is equivalent to *in unum*, and it is occasionally used in this literal sense, " into one," meaning " together." Thus in John 11, 52, " that he might gather *together* the children of God who were scattered," the Syriac versions have *laḥdā* (Greek εἰς ἕν). Similarly in John 17, 23, " that they (the believers) may be perfected *together* " (lit. *into one*; Greek as above), the Palestinian Syriac has *laḥdā*, while the Lewis and Peshitta versions have *leḥad*. A good example of the use of the word to mean " together," Heb. יחדו, is found in the Palestinian Syriac version of Is. 43, 17: " Who bringeth out chariots and horses, host and hero *together* (לחדא)." *But in the Judean dialects of Aramaic the usual meaning of* לחדא *is* " *greatly, exceedingly,*" *and this is pre-*

*cisely what is needed in the place of* ἐπὶ τὸ αὐτό *in Acts 2, 47.* For example, in the Onkelos Targum לַחְדָא (properly " singularly, uniquely ") is the ordinary rendering of Heb. מְאֹד . Thus, Exod. 19, 18, " And the whole mountain trembled greatly," וְזָע כָּל טוּרָא לַחְדָא . Similarly in Palestinian Syriac, the Judean dialect as we find it several centuries later (c. 5th cent. A.D.): Matt. 2, 16, " Then Herod . . . was angered exceedingly (*laḥdā*)." Examples with verbs of multiplying, increasing, and the like are numerous; thus from the Onk. Targ.: Gen. 17, 2, " I will multiply thee exceedingly (לַחְדָא לַחְדָא, corresponding to Heb. מְאֹד מְאֹד); Exod. 1, 7, "The children of Israel grew in strength exceedingly "; and many others. It is also worthy of especial notice that in the clauses where this adverb modifies a verb it is regularly placed *at the end of the clause* — like the ἐπὶ τὸ αὐτό in the verse under consideration.

At the end of Acts 2 the statement that the church " was *greatly* increased daily " is certainly to be expected; not only because of the way in which similar statements are interjected at frequent intervals through all this part of the history (4, 4; 5, 14; 6, 7; 9, 31), but also in particular because comparison of 2, 41 with 4, 4 shows that this writer did indeed think of this very time as one in which the company of believers was *greatly* and *rapidly* increased. We know that it was not his habit to understate.

The question why the Greek translator misunderstood his text, can be answered with greater ease and certainty than is ordinarily possible in explaining supposed mistranslations. The reason is simply this, that the use of לַחְדָא to mean "greatly," etc., is a peculiarity of the Judean dialect, while the Greek version was presumably made at some distance from Judea. This use of the word is not only absolutely unknown in the Aramaic of Northern Syria and in classical Syriac, but it is also unheard of in the other Palestinian dialects, including even the Galilean. It is never found, for instance, in the Palestinian Talmud or Midrash (Dalman, *Grammatik des jüdisch-palästinischen Aramäisch*,[2] 211).[1] If we suppose, for example, that this document of the Jerusalem church, composed in

---

[1] For an instance of this usage in a remote Aramaic dialect, see Nöldeke, *Mandäische Grammatik*, 207 below.

Judea, was translated by a native of Antioch, familiar with Aramaic from his childhood, we can scarcely doubt that on coming to לחדא he would be somewhat puzzled by it. It could hardly suggest to him, in this context, any other idea than "together," and we should expect him to render it by the customary phrase ἐπὶ τὸ αὐτό.

We may then restore the original Aramaic of 2, 47b as follows: וּמָרְיָא[1] מוֹסֵף הֲוָא לְדִי חָיֵין כָּל יוֹם לַחְדָא. Here, the preposition ל in the fourth word might signify either the dative or the direct object. Doubtless it was originally intended to signify the former; but if the translator failed to recognize the peculiar use of לחדא (and we certainly should not expect him, if he lived at a distance from Judea, to be familiar with this merely local idiom), it was inevitable that he should render with the Greek accusative. The correct rendering would be: ὁ δὲ κύριος προσετίθει τοῖς σωζομένοις καθ' ἡμέραν σφόδρα, "And the Lord added greatly day by day to the saved."[2]

The argument derived from this passage is exceedingly forcible. The hypothesis of accidental coincidence would be difficult enough even if we had only this one case to consider. But the fact is, as will be seen, that half a dozen others, hardly less striking, are to be put beside it. Even the evidence that author and translator lived in different parts of the Aramaic-speaking world receives corroboration from other passages.

3, 16. Καὶ ἐπὶ τῇ πίστει τοῦ ὀνόματος αὐτοῦ τοῦτον ὃν θεωρεῖτε καὶ οἴδατε ἐστερέωσεν τὸ ὄνομα αὐτοῦ καὶ ἡ πίστις ἡ δι' αὐτοῦ ἔδωκεν αὐτῷ τὴν ὁλοκληρίαν ταύτην ἀπέναντι πάντων ὑμῶν. "And by faith in his name hath *his name* made this man strong, whom ye see and know; yea, the faith which is through him hath given him this perfect soundness before you all."

The passage presents two very obvious and serious difficulties. In the first place, the mode of expression is intolerably awkward and

---

[1] I use this word (מָרְיָא or מָרְאָה, מָרָא) simply for convenience, since we cannot be certain what Aramaic original is rendered by ὁ κύριος in this and similar passages. The Aramaic-speaking Christians of the early church in Judea presumably followed the current Jewish usage. On the latter, see Dalman, *Worte Jesu*, 346 ff., 266 ff.

[2] Lit., "those that *were living*," i. e., were in the way of life; σώζεσθαι is the standing Greek equivalent of this verb, as also σωτηρία of the noun חַיִּין; see the Syriac versions of the Bible.

confused, in Greek even more than in English. Wendt, *Komm.*, attempts to account for " die Schwerfälligkeit des Ausdrucks," but does not succeed in showing any good reason for it. On the contrary, the ideas which he supposes to have been intended could very easily have been put into palatable Greek even by a writer of moderate ability. Why, in particular, was it necessary to obscure the sense and spoil the sound by the ugly repetition of τὸ ὄνομα αὐτοῦ? The second difficulty is far more important, namely this, that the passage — that is, the first half of verse 16 — is out of keeping with its own context. By what power was the cripple healed? The whole surrounding context implies that it was the power of Jesus, and the latter half of this same verse 16 says that " the *faith* which is through *him* " made the man whole. But 16a expressly attributes the healing to a certain quasi-magical power in *the Name* of Jesus. As Preuschen (*in loc.*) says, " Der Name wirkt selbst das Wunder." Such an outcropping bit of popular superstition (not found elsewhere in the New Testament) might indeed be credited to the author of this narrative if the evidence of it were unequivocal, but in point of fact the evidence is confined to this one curious and clumsy half-verse. We certainly seem to see here the power of the Name itself expressly distinguished from the power of faith in or through the name; but on the other hand in 3, 26; 4, 2, 10*b*, 11, 12*a*; 5, 31; 10, 38 we read only of the power of Jesus, and in 3, 16*b* of the power of faith through him. No wonder Preuschen wishes to cancel 16*b* as an interpolation, made " um der Stellung gerecht zu werden, die sonst der Glaube bei den Heilungen einnimmt." It is one thing to say that the healing is performed " in the name of Jesus " (3, 6; 4, 10*a*, 12*b*, 30), or " through his name " (10, 43), or " through faith in his name " (3, 16, beginning), but quite another thing to say that *the name itself, through faith in it,* wrought the miracle![1]

[1] It is evidently under the influence of 3, 16a that so many modern interpreters refer τούτῳ in 4, 10 to the name, rather than to Jesus himself. Wendt, *Komm.*, declares this to be " grammatisch genauer "; it is, however, rather a question of rhetoric than of grammar. To me, at least, the whole passage sounds better and more like the author of this narrative when the transition from the name to the person is made at just this point. Observe how the very same transition, in the reverse order, ἐν ἄλλῳ οὐδενί . . . ἐν ᾧ (τῷ ὀνόματι), is made two verses farther on, in vs. 12.

Turning the Greek word by word into Aramaic we obtain the following result: ובהימנתא די שְׁמֵהּ להדן די חזין אנתון וידעין אנתון תקף שמה והימנתא די בה יהבת לה חלימותא דא קדם כלכון. Here there is a curious ambiguity in the middle of the sentence, which probably accounts for the difficulty in our Greek. What was originally intended was not תַּקֵּף שְׁמֵהּ, ἐστερέωσε τὸ ὄνομα αὐτοῦ, but תַּקֵּף שְׁמֵהּ ὑγιῆ ἐποίησεν (or κατέστησεν) αὐτόν. This latter phrase is idiomatic in all respects, and suits its context perfectly, the subject of the verb being either Ἰησοῦς or ὁ θεός.[1] Luke's rendering is a very natural one, since he seemed to have before him the same word (שְׁמֵהּ) which he had rendered at the beginning of the sentence. The translation should then be: "*And by faith in His name He hath made strong this one whom ye see and know; yea, the faith which is through Him hath given him this soundness before you all.*" Compare with the verse as thus restored 10, 43, which is a good parallel. Notice also that the Syriac version renders in this same way, "*He hath made sound and whole*," apparently cutting loose from the Greek and translating according to the requirement of the context. 9, 34, 40 also show plainly (what no one would question, but for this mistranslated passage) that the miracles of healing, and even of restoration of the dead to life, were performed through faith in Jesus, indeed, but *not* by his name.

**4, 24 ff.** Δέσποτα, σὺ ὁ ποιήσας τὸν οὐρανὸν καὶ τὴν γῆν καὶ τὴν θάλασσαν καὶ πάντα τὰ ἐν αὐτοῖς, ὁ τοῦ πατρὸς ἡμῶν διὰ πνεύματος ἁγίου στόματος Δαυεὶδ παιδός σου εἰπών· ἵνα τί ἐφρύαξαν ἔθνη . . . καὶ κατὰ τοῦ Χριστοῦ αὐτοῦ. συνήχθησαν γὰρ κ.τ.ἑ. The difficulty of this passage, namely of *the first clause of verse 25*, is so notorious that it need not be set forth here. It is sufficient to say that modern scholars have either virtually or expressly declared the text quite hopeless. It is not merely that the whole clause ὁ τοῦ πατρὸς ἡμῶν . . . εἰπών is untranslatable — an incoherent jumble of words; the fact is quite as noticeable that no simple emendation of the Greek will render the clause intelligible. The problem is not to be solved by cancelling words, nor by adding them, nor by making transposi-

---

[1] In the Greek, the latter would be preferred. Not so in Semitic, in which the change of subject is easier. Cf. also 9, 34.

tions. The clumsy phrase which Wendt (*Komm.*, p. 115, note 2) hesitatingly accepts as the possible original was not obtained by any scientific process, but simply by cutting loose — as some of the early versions did — from the text which has been handed down to us. Preuschen says very truly that the words which constitute the first clause of vs. 25 "spotten jeden Versuches einer Konstruktion" (or, he might have added, Rekonstruktion). He himself regards τοῦ πατρὸς ἡμῶν and διὰ πνεύματος ἁγίου as glosses, but this explanation is quite without plausibility; the former phrase (a most unlikely addition) would never have been placed where it now stands, and as for the latter, it is so superfluous as to be all but inconceivable as a gloss. The fact is, our Greek text of the verse is extremely well attested, and no attempt to get beyond it has ever succeeded.

As soon as the question of an underlying Aramaic idiom is raised, the probability suggests itself that the source of the confusion lay in a relative clause beginning היא די אבונא, "*that which* our father . . .," which was misread as הוא די אבונא, ὁ τοῦ πατρὸς ἡμῶν. Turning the Greek back into Aramaic we obtain: היא די אבונא לפום רוחא די קודשא דויד עברך אמר, "*That which our father, thy servant David, said by* (or, *by the command of*) *the Holy Spirit*"; etc. It is obvious that the neuter pronoun, "that which," is required by the whole passage: the connection of the address Δέσποτα . . . αὐτοῖς becomes evident for the first time, and the γάρ in vs. 27 now comes to its own. Instead of the more common לפום, כפום[1] might have been used; compare e.g. כפי יהוה, "by the command of Yahwè," 1 Chron. 12, 23. In the order of words in this restored Aramaic there is nothing unusual; such delayed apposition is of frequent occurrence, and in this case we can see a rhetorical reason for separating "our father" from "thy servant David." There is now no ellipsis in the passage,[2] but everything is expressed as clearly and naturally as possible. But as soon as the י of היא was lengthened into ו (perhaps the most common of all accidents in Hebrew-Aramaic manuscripts, and here made especially easy by the preceding context) the whole passage was

---

[1] For the Greek rendering, cf. διὰ στόματος for לפי in 1 Kings 17, 1; an excellent parallel.

[2] In English idiom we should use *as* instead of *that which*: "Why (as our father David said) do the heathen rage?"

ruined. הוא די אבונא was of necessity ὁ τοῦ πατρὸς ἡμῶν, and every other part of our Greek text followed inevitably; there is no other way in which a faithful translator would have been likely to render it.[1]

This passage gives exceedingly strong support to the theory of translation. The manner in which the change from י to ו reduces perfect order to complete chaos is as remarkable as anything of the sort in the history of the ancient versions.

**8, 10.** This passage occurs in the story of Simon the Sorcerer. He by his sorcery had made such an impression on the people of his city that they all united in saying: Οὗτός ἐστιν ἡ δύναμις τοῦ θεοῦ ἡ καλουμένη μεγάλη, which must be translated: "This (man) is the power of God which is called great." Both ancient and modern scholars have been perplexed by this sentence. Some Greek manuscripts and early versions, including the Peshitta, omit καλουμένη as superfluous — and so indeed it is. Preuschen would cancel it. But how, then, account for its presence in our text? There is no conceivable reason why it should have been added. As for the "*great* power," it has been pointed out (what we could have taken for granted even without the demonstration) that Gnostic formulae and magic texts speak of a μεγάλη δύναμις. But this is quite outside the atmosphere of the Book of Acts; nor have we any reason whatever for supposing that the people of Samaria were a Gnostic community. Some, including Wendt, have even preferred to follow Klostermann's curious suggestion that the μεγάλη of this verse was originally a transliteration of מְגַלֵּא "revealing!"

But the main difficulty of the verse, after all, lies in the τοῦ θεοῦ. Who, or what, can have been intended by this phrase? It is tolerably certain that the scene of these events is the capital city of the province Samaria, i.e. Sebaste.[2] Now it is well known, though often

---

[1] The manner of the translator in sticking close to a difficult Semitic text, following word by word the order of the original (excepting that he did not, of course, write διὰ στόματος πνεύματος), is the same which we see in Luke 1 and 2; see *Aramaic Gospels*, pp. 292 ff., 305.

[2] If we had only verse 5 to deal with, we should hardly hesitate to declare the rather noticeable phrase ἡ πόλις τῆς Σαμαρίας a mistranslation of מדינת שמרין, "the *province* of Samaria"; cf. Luke 1, 39, where the mistranslation is certain. In verses 9

forgotten, that *the city* (earlier Samaria, later Sebaste) was never a seat of the " Samaritan " religion. Aside from Shechem-Neapolis — always the headquarters — the sect occupied certain towns and districts of the province, but never the capital city; " die Stadt Samarien blieb heidnisch, und gehörte nicht zu der Gemeinde der Samariter " (Wellhausen, *Israelitische und jüdische Geschichte*,[1] 194; see also his *Kritische Analyse*," 14). We must therefore suppose that those to whom Philip was preaching were polytheists; not foreigners, indeed, but the result of a mixture of nations and a syncretism of religions which contained Israelite elements; men who believed in gods many and lords many. What deity could the people of Sebaste have designated as ὁ θεός?

Verse 10b rendered into Aramaic reads as follows: דֵּין חֵילָא דִי אֱלָהָא דִי מִתְקְרֵא רַב. This is grammatically ambiguous as it stands, seeing that the gender of חיל happens to be masculine; but it is beyond question that the rendering required by all that we know of the situation is the following: αὕτη (οὗτος is also possible) ἐστὶν ἡ δύναμις τοῦ θεοῦ τοῦ καλουμένου μεγάλου, "*This is the power of the God who is called Great.*" It is true, in the first place, that both Jewish and early Christian usage gave to God the title Μέγας; see for example Sir. 39, 6; 43, 28; 3 Macc. 7, 22; Titus 2, 13. In early Syriac *rabbā*, ὁ Μέγας, is occasionally used absolutely as his title. Jews employ this adjective in speaking of their God to foreigners; thus Daniel says to Nebuchadnezzar (2, 45): " A Great God (Greek, ὁ θεὸς ὁ μέγας) has made known to the king what shall come to pass," and in Bel and the Dragon 41 the foreign king confesses: Μέγας ἐστὶ Κύριος ὁ θεός. Again, in the Book of Acts we not only see a " great " god distinguished from other gods (19, 27 f.), but we also have in 16, 17 a virtual parallel to the present passage, inasmuch as the superiority of the Christians' God is confessed by a foreigner: the clairvoyant maid of Philippi declares Paul and his companions to be " servants of the *Most High* (ὑψίστου) God." [1] In

and 14 Σαμαρία is of course the province (ἔθνος in 9 is probably an inaccurate rendering of עַם " people "), but 8 and 9 sound rather as though a city were really intended.

[1] Cf. also such passages as those quoted by Norden, *Agnostos Theos* 39 f.: εἷς μὲν ὁ μέγιστος καὶ καθυπέρτερος καὶ ὁ κρατέων τοῦ παντός, τοὶ δ'ἄλλοι πολλοὶ διαφέροντες κατὰ δύναμιν (from the " Onatas " cited by Stobaeus); εἷς θεός, ἔν τε θεοῖσι καὶ ἀνθρώ-

a word, the phrase " the God who is called Great " is a thoroughly suitable one for this context, from any point of view. Luke the translator, led by his own monotheism rather than by his imagination, erred in connecting the adjective with the word " power."

**11, 27–30.** This passage is one of the most satisfactory of all, in the proof of translation which it affords. Certain prophets had come from Jerusalem to Antioch. One of them, named Agabus, made a formal (ἀναστάς) prediction of an approaching famine. Verse 28 says of this: ἐσήμαινεν διὰ τοῦ πνεύματος λιμὸν μεγάλην μέλλειν ἔσεσθαι ἐφ' ὅλην τὴν οἰκουμένην· ἥτις ἐγένετο ἐπὶ Κλαυδίου, "He signified by the Spirit that there would be a great famine *upon all the world*; which came to pass in the days of Claudius." Verses 29 f. then proceed to tell how, when the famine came, *the disciples in Antioch, every man according to his ability, sent relief to the brethren in Judea.* That is, there was no famine in Antioch, and the narrator seems to have in mind only Judea as the afflicted region. Josephus, *Antt.* xx, 5, 2 (cf. 2, 5), does indeed tell of a " great famine " which came upon Judea in the first years of the reign of Claudius.

There have been many attempts to explain the passage. Some, like Schürer, *Gesch.*[3], I, 567, note 8, would pronounce the statement in verse 28 " eine ungeschichtliche Generalisirung." But that is obviously not the case, if verses 29 f. refer to the same famine; the region of Antioch was not affected. Preuschen and others, misled by the fact that Roman writers mention local famines in several parts of the empire (but none of them at all wide-spread, nor any one affecting Palestine except the one above mentioned) in the reign of Claudius, decide that a widely extended famine was indeed correctly foretold by Agabus, in verse 28, but that in verses 29 f. this famine is confounded with the one in Judea described by Josephus; see also *Encycl. Bibl.*, art. " Chronology," § 76, where the facts are

ποισι μέγιστος (from Xenophanes); ... ὑμνεῖν θεούς, ἐφ' ἅπασι δὲ ἤδη τὸν μέγαν τῶν ἐκεῖ βασιλέα καὶ ἐν τῷ πλήθει μάλιστα τῶν θεῶν τὸ μέγα αὐτοῦ ἐνδεικνυμένους (from Plotinus); and finally, in the passage quoted from Apollonius of Tyana: ... θεῷ μέν, ὃν δὴ πρῶτον ἔφαμεν, κ.τ.λ., and at the end of the passage: οὐκοῦν κατὰ ταῦτα οὐδαμῶς τῷ μεγάλῳ καὶ ἐπὶ πάντων θεῷ θύτεον. "The God who is called Great" was an idea familiar to both Greeks and Semites in the days of the Apostles. But Luke's translation is a perfectly natural one.

stated not quite accurately. This is certainly a desperate attempt at explanation. Wendt concludes that the author of Acts here misunderstood his source; the words of Agabus were originally intended as a prophecy of " hunger for the word of the Lord " (Amos 8, 11), but were mistakenly supposed to predict a famine! It is certainly difficult to imagine the nature of a " source " in which the context would not show which sort of famine was intended by the prophet.

But the explanation of the difficulty is both easy and sure. The Aramaic original had the word אַרְעָא ( = Heb. אֶרֶץ, "land, earth"). The author of this document, writing in Jerusalem, followed the time-honored usage in calling Judea simply " *the land.*" But when the translator, living outside Palestine, came to the phrase כל ארעא, it was only natural that he should render it by ὅλη ἡ οἰκουμένη, " all the earth." It is a mistake that has been made a great many times. Luke himself made it, in exactly the same way, in his Gospel 2, 1 (*Aramaic Gospels*, p. 293), where he represented Quirinius as taxing " all the world " (πᾶσαν τὴν οἰκουμένην = כל הארץ) instead of " all the land " of Palestine.

15, 7. The beginning of the speech of Peter in the council at Jerusalem: Ἄνδρες ἀδελφοί, ὑμεῖς ἐπίστασθε ὅτι ἀφ' ἡμερῶν ἀρχαίων ἐν ὑμῖν ἐξελέξατο ὁ θεὸς διὰ τοῦ στόματός μου ἀκοῦσαι τὰ ἔθνη τὸν λόγον τοῦ εὐαγγελίου καὶ πιστεῦσαι. This presents at least three considerable problems. Ἐν ὑμῖν is obscure, and its connection uncertain. Many, including Preuschen, prefer to read ἐν ἡμῖν, which, however, does not do away with the main difficulty. Some texts, including the Peshitta and Sahidic versions, prefer to omit the troublesome words altogether. Again, the verb ἐξελέξατο is hanging in the air, without any direct object. In order to see how hopeless the case really is, read the comment of Wendt (*Komm.*, pp. 228 f.). He finally suggests, with some hesitation, that although the infinitive clause is dependent on the idea of " choosing " in the sense of *beschliessen*, yet instead of such a verb the author preferred to substitute one meaning *wählen*, since Peter had in fact been " selected " for this work. But did not Luke know the Greek language? If he meant εὐδόκησεν, why did he not write it? and if he wished to speak of the selection of an evangelist to the heathen, why did he not do so intelligibly, giving his verb a direct object? Finally, the phrase ἀφ' ἡμερῶν ἀρχαίων is ridiculously unsuitable in this connection. As the text stands, the reference can only be to the events of chap. 10, which happened only a few years before the time of the council. Preuschen calls the phrase a "starker Ausdruck für πρότερον." But the two expressions mean very different things! Why, if Luke meant "formerly" or "recently," did he write "from days of old"?[1]

The Aramaic equivalent of the troublesome passage would read thus: אנתון ידעתון די מן יומי עלמא בכון בחר אלהא למשמע עממיא על פומי מלתא די בסורתא ולהימנא. This is both idiomatic and unambiguous. בכון stands before the verb for the sake of emphasis, and the reason of the emphasis is obvious. It was an important question, whether the evangelizing of the Gentiles, which had made so portentous a beginning, was a thing which had arisen far from Jerusalem and without the coöperation of the Apostles to whom Jesus had committed the charge of his church. The Greek follows the Aramaic with absolute fidelity; so closely, in fact, that the result is a mistranslation. The verb בחר is construed with ב, which is replaced by ἐν; compare Luke 12, 8, ὃς ἂν ὁμολογήσῃ ἐν ἐμοί, "whoever confesses me," and many similar cases. Perhaps if the בכון had been placed after the verb, Luke would not have rendered so cautiously.[2] The rendering in English is: "*Ye know that from of old God chose you, that the Gentiles might hear, by my mouth, the word of the gospel, and believe.*" In this sentence Peter reminds his hearers of two things: first, that Israel, and therefore the Church of the Messiah, had been chosen to give light to the Gentiles; and again, that he himself had begun this work, having been the first to bring to them the gifts of baptism and the Holy Spirit. But the emphasis is put, in the Aramaic, on the pronoun "*you*," and the mission of the elect church which is the salt of the earth, rather than on Peter and the incident of his initial effort.

[1] Compare ἐκ γενεῶν ἀρχαίων in this same chapter, vs. 21.

[2] It is of course to be borne in mind that a translator who follows his original rather closely is more likely to make mistakes in translating Aramaic than in rendering Hebrew or Arabic, because of the greater freedom in the order of words in the Aramaic sentence.

## § 4. Other Evidence of Translation in these Chapters

Aside from the instances of serious mistranslation, the following passages containing further evidence may be pointed out.

1, 1. Ἤρξατο is simply the usual rendering of Aram. שָׁרֵי, which in the Palestinian dialect is used constantly in this almost redundant way (see e.g. Dalman, *Worte Jesu*, 21 f.). It is very unlikely that the word would have been used here in a Greek composition.[1] See also below.

1, 2. The awkward position of διὰ πνεύματος ἁγίου (Wellhausen, *Analyse*, would cancel the phrase as a later addition) is another result of translation. In the Aramaic, the words came at the end of the sentence, just before the verb (ἀνελήμφθη). But in that position it might refer to *either one of the two phrases*, " giving commandment to the Apostles " and " whom he had chosen." The only way a cautious translator could preserve this ambiguity was to put the words where they now stand.

1, 4. It is probable that the somewhat unusual word συναλιζόμενος is the (exact) rendering of Aramaic מִתְמַלַּח, this *ithpaʿal* meaning primarily " eat salt in company with," and then simply " have (table-) companionship with." The *peʿal* occurs in the Old Testament, Ezra 4, 14: " We have been guests (literally *have eaten the salt*) of the palace." The *ithpaʿal* happens to be known to us only in the northern (Syriac) dialect, but it must have been in use in the Palestinian speech. Typical examples in Syriac are the following. Ps. 140, 4 (Heb. 141, 4): " I will not *break bread* with them (wicked men)," where Hebrew has the denominative אלחם. *St. Ephraemi opera*, ed. Overbeck, 300, 19: " Now let us *be his guests at table* " ; said by Joseph's brethren, Gen. 43, 32–34. *Ephr. Syr. opera*, ed. Benedictus, i, 474 A: " He (Jeroboam) *consorted* with a heathen people "; where the context, which is concerned with idolatry, shows that the author had in mind primarily sacrificial feasts. *Ibid.*, 534 C: " With sinners he (Jesus) *consorted* and ate "; the two verbs being all but synonymous. Finally, the verb is used in the Harklean Syriac rendering of συναλιζόμενος in this passage.

[1] For a conjecture as to the beginning of the Aramaic document, see below.

It is certainly easy, then, to regard the Greek word as a translation. As to the meaning of the original Aramaic here there could be no doubt. The distinct character of the word, the use of the corresponding form in Syriac, and the emphasis laid in the oldest Christian tradition on the fact that the risen Jesus ate with his disciples (March 16, 14; Luke 24, 30, 40 ff.; Acts 10, 41; John 21, 9–13), all combine to show that *eating with them* was the meaning intended. It is plain, moreover, that we have here in verses 3–8 a series of allusions to the narrative in Luke 24, 36–49; see further below.

1, 4. The transition to direct discourse, in just this manner, is the usual thing in Aramaic.

1, 5. For the redundant demonstrative (ταύτας) in Jewish Aramaic, see Dalman, *Gramm.*² 113 f.

1, 6. Οἱ συνελθόντες is of course "those who had come together," or better "those who were present." In Aramaic, די מתכנשין הוו.

1, 18. Note the possibility that πρηνὴς γενόμενος renders נפל, and that in the original Aramaic the word meant "*cast himself down.*" The whole verse may well have read as follows: הָדֵן דִּי קְנָא חַקְלָא מִן אַגְרָא דִּי חֲטָאָה וּנְפַל וְאִתְבְּזַע מִן מְצִיעָא וְכָל מְעוֹהִי אִתְאֲשָׁדוּ. "For he had purchased a field with his ill-gotten gain; and having cast himself down, he burst asunder in the middle, and all his bowels gushed out." This is strikingly summary; it would seem that the narrator had no relish for the tale of Judas' death, but made it as brief as he could. It was well known to all those for whom he was writing; on the other hand, not every one of them knew the origin of the local name "*Ḥaqel-dᵃmā*," and it was chiefly in order to put this on record that he introduced here the parenthesis (vss. 18, 19). For the ambiguity of נפל, cf. especially the Lewis Syr. rendering of Matt. 4, 6: βάλε σεαυτὸν κάτω, *pel men hāmekkā*; also John 21, 7: Peter girt his coat about him, and *cast himself* (ἔβαλεν ἑαυτόν, *nᵉphal*) into the sea.[1] This ambiguity could easily account for the Greek of Acts 1, 18. The local tradition was unquestionably this, that Judas committed

---

[1] Cf. further the Syriac renderings of Matt. 3, 10 (Lew., Pesh.); 5, 29 (Pesh.); 21, 21 (Lew., Cur., Pesh.); Mark 11, 20 (Lew., Pesh.); Luke 3, 9 (Lew., Cur., Pesh.), in all of which βάλλεσθαι, *passive*, is rendered simply by נפל.

suicide. The translation πρηνὴς γενόμενος left room for this, as the use of πίπτειν would not have done. The Greek is not difficult, cf. κατὰ γῆν γενόμενος, 2 Macc. 9, 8, in the story of the death of Antiochus Epiphanes. It is hardly necessary to insist that πρηνής does not mean, and could not mean, "swollen"! The fanciful expansion of the story found in Papias was the source of the Armenian translation in this passage, as well as of the Armenian and Latin (πρηνεῖς rendered *inflatos*) in Wisd. 4, 19.[1] The account of the death of Judas in Acts is not derived from the passage in Wisdom (Preuschen, p. 8); it is not surprising, on the other hand, that *after Acts 1–15 had been translated into Greek* many should have been reminded by it of the words ῥήξει . . . πρηνεῖς in the older passage — though the resemblance is not in any way remarkable. Nor does it seem to be the case that Matt. follows another tradition ("einer völlig abweichenden Ueberlieferung," Preuschen, *ibid.*). The author of the First Gospel starts from the same popular belief regarding the "Field of Blood,"[2] but makes out of it his own story, *more suo*, on the basis of Zech. 11, 12 f. There is nothing improbable in the supposition that Judas owned a piece of land, and committed suicide on it; nor that the "Field of Blood" actually received its name in this way.

1, 22. "During all the time that the Lord Jesus went in and out among us, ἀρξάμενος ἀπὸ τοῦ βαπτίσματος Ἰωάνου ἕως τῆς ἡμέρας ἧς ἀνελήμφθη ἀφ' ἡμῶν." This is an Aramaic idiom: "from (מִשְׁרָא מִן)[3] . . . unto (עַד)." Similarly Matt. 20, 8, ἀρξάμενος ἀπὸ τῶν ἐσχάτων ἕως τῶν πρώτων; Luke 23, 5, διδάσκων καθ' ὅλης τῆς Ἰουδαίας, καὶ ἀρξάμενος ἀπὸ τῆς Γαλιλαίας ἕως ὧδε. This is passable Greek, though not classical (Blass § 74, 2); but the verb, or participle,

[1] Acute disease of the bowels, in one form or another, is a strikingly common feature of oriental popular accounts of "the most miserable death of the wicked." Aside from the story in 2 Macc. 9, that of the death of Herod the Great in Jos., *Antt.* xvii, 6, 5, *Bell. Jud.* i, 33, 5, and of Herod Agrippa I in Acts 12, 23, compare the accounts of abdomens bursting, bowels consumed by fire, or by worms, and the like, in the ancient Life of Simeon Stylites (*Journal of the Am. Or. Soc.*, 36, pp. 49, 56, 57, 69, 70; cf. also 53).

[2] Whether the ἀπήγξατο, "hanged himself," of Matt. 27, 5 belonged to the tradition, or was merely Matthew's inexact term for the mode of suicide, may be questioned.

[3] וּמִשְׁרָא, or בְּדִי מִשְׁרָא, might equally well be used.

of "beginning" is one which is often used loosely in Palestinian Aramaic, even to the point of redundance (see the note on 1, 1), and it seems plain that what we have here is a form of this local peculiarity. In several other passages (see below) the Greek participle ἀρξάμενος is used in this same way; and from a comparison of all the occurrences, with especial regard to the structure of the sentence in each case, it becomes increasingly probable that a peculiar idiomatic use of מְשָׁרֵא is the source of our Greek. In Aramaic the word is an accusative of state or condition,[1] sometimes rather loosely connected, so that a faithful Greek rendering is likely to be awkward. Even in Luke 23, 5 (just cited) the clause sounds decidedly better when turned into Aramaic.[2] In Luke 24, 27 we seem to have an example of the looser use of the native idiom: "And then (ἀρξάμενος) from Moses and all the prophets he interpreted to them," etc. In two other passages with ἀρξάμενος we see exemplified in a very striking way Luke's cautious faithfulness, leading him into translation-Greek of the stiffest type. The first of these is Luke 24, 47: "It is written ... that repentance and remission of sins should be preached (κηρυχθῆναι) in his name unto all the nations (εἰς πάντα τὰ ἔθνη), ἀρξάμενοι ἀπὸ Ἰερουσαλήμ. ὑμεῖς μάρτυρες τούτων." The Aramaic could have precisely this participial construction, the participle being in the accusative of condition, though without case-ending or other sign to show how it should be connected: וְדִי תִסְתַּבַּר בִּשְׁמֵהּ תְּיוּבָה לִשְׁבִיקוּת חֲטָאִין לְכָל עַמְמַיָּא מְשָׁרֵין מִן יְרוּשְׁלֵם אַנְתּוּן סָהֲדִין דִּי אִלֵּין. Here, the participle "beginning" should be connected with "the nations"; it *might*, however, by a loose construction, be referred to *the disciples*; and since the next following words are "ye are witnesses," while the very next verse (49) commands the disciples to remain in the city for the present (cf. Acts 1, 4, 8, etc.), and they did in fact begin preaching to the Gentiles in Jerusalem, it is probable that any good translator of that

---

[1] A favorite construction with the participle in the Semitic languages; cf. e. g., Ezr. 7, 16 מתנדבין, Targ. Is. 53, 7 בָּעֵי; in Hebrew, 1 Ki. 14, 6 באה, Hag. 1, 3 ספונים; and with prefixed וְ, 2 Sam. 13, 20 וְשֹׁמֵמָה, Hab. 2, 10 וחוטא. Examples could be multiplied to any extent.

[2] Cod. D gives the Greek a more natural sound by omitting the καί, whose use is not justified by the context. In Aramaic the וְ is entirely idiomatic, see above.

time would have chosen ἀρξάμενοι rather than ἀρξάμενα. The Greek was bound to be bad in either case, and the masculine made better sense.

The other passage is Acts 10, 37: ὑμεῖς οἴδατε τὸ γενόμενον ῥῆμα καθ' ὅλης τῆς Ἰουδαίας, ἀρξάμενος ἀπὸ τῆς Γαλιλαίας μετὰ τὸ βάπτισμα ὃ ἐκήρυξεν Ἰωάνης, Ἰησοῦν τὸν ἀπὸ Ναζαρέθ, ὡς ἔχρισεν αὐτὸν ὁ θεὸς πνεύματι ἁγίῳ καὶ δυνάμει, ὃς διῆλθεν εὐεργετῶν κ.τ.λ. This case very closely resembles the other. There was the same Aramaic particple, משרא, in the same construction: אנתון ידעין אנתון פתגמא די הוא בכל יהוד משרא מן גלילא . . . ישוע נצריא די משחה אלהא וכו' Of course the obvious connection of the participle is with פתגמא (ῥῆμα, "thing"); yet in view of Acts 1, 22, Ἰησοῦς ἀρξάμενος ἀπὸ τοῦ βαπτίσματος Ἰωάνου, and Luke 23, 5, καὶ ἀρξάμενος ἀπὸ τῆς Γαλιλαίας (!), the translator must have felt it important to leave open the possibility that here also, as in the two parallel passages, it was Jesus who "began." The only way in which he could do this, while keeping close to his original, was to use the masculine nominative case, ἀρξάμενος. It is a very common translator's device, illustrated in the Greek O.T. as well as in the Book of Revelation in the N.T.[1]

Blass, § 31, 6 (end), thought that ἀρξάμενος ἀπὸ τῆς Γαλιλαίας in Acts 10, 37 might have been interpolated from Luke 23, 5. From what source, then, was ἀρξάμενοι ἀπὸ Ἱερουσαλήμ in Luke 24, 47 interpolated? The two cases explain and support each other unmistakably; in both the correct text has been preserved along with later attempts at improvement. The twofold barbarism is not due to a twofold accident, it is simply a well-known feature of translation Greek. The man who composed Luke 1, 1–4 (and, as I believe, also Acts 16–28) knew the Greek language, had ideas regarding literary style, and was capable of expressing himself clearly in a way that was not intolerably clumsy. But the ancient translator

---

[1] Compare also with both these passages such cases as 1 Ki. 5, 14: καὶ ἀπέστειλεν αὐτοὺς εἰς τὸν Λίβανον, δέκα χιλιάδες ἐν τῷ μηνί, ἀλλασσόμενοι· μῆνα ἦσαν ἐν τῷ Λιβάνῳ, κ.τ.λ. Here the participle is masculine, not feminine, because חליפות refers rather to the suffix prounoun (= αὐτοὺς) than to אלפים; and nominative because of the liberty which the *translator* enjoys (observe that in the original the case is the same suspended accusative of condition which we have in our ἀρξάμενος passages).

was under a compulsion stronger than that of style. From the point of view of his time, there was no way of solving this particular problem of interpretation more satisfactory than the one which he chose.

2, 1. An interesting and characteristic specimen of translation. "When the day of Pentecost *arrived*," but neither συμπληροῦσθαι nor any Semitic equivalent can mean this. Moreover, "Pentecost," ἡ ἡμέρα τῆς πεντηκοστῆς, is a Hellenistic coinage. Obviously, the original was: וּבְמִשְׁלַם שָׁבוּעַיָּא, "and when the Weeks were fulfilled," i.e., the seven weeks intervening before the Feast. It was customary to refer to the interval in just this way, see e.g. Num. 28, 26. Luke, always faithful and always Hellenistic, rendered the infinitive exactly (the same translation in Luke 9, 51), but employed the technical terminology which his readers would understand.

2, 7. Οὐχὶ ἰδού reproduces לָא הָא. The Aramaic interjection is inserted very often for emphasis where הנה or הן would not be used in Hebrew. This use in interrogation (*nonne*) is known to us mainly from classical Syriac; cf. the Peshitta in Matt. 24, 2, etc. It is also good Arabic.

2, 22. "Designated *by* (ἀπό) God." מן is very frequently used with a passive verb to denote the agent; 4, 36, and 15, 33 are similar cases. Cf. also Luke 6, 18; 7, 35!

2, 24. It has long been recognized that this verse contains an ancient mistranslation, inasmuch as the LXX's ὠδῖνες θανάτου in Ps. 17, 5; 144, 3 is a false rendering of חבלי מות, "*bands* of death." But scholars have failed to draw the necessary conclusion from λύσας, which, as many have observed, suits only the "bands," not the "pains." No writer composing his own Greek would ever have chosen this unsuitable word, and there is nothing in the Old Testament that could have led him to employ it. The appeal sometimes made to Job 39, 2 (LXX) is not justified, for that grotesquely confused passage is as far removed as possible from the ideas with which the author of Acts is here dealing. Three verbs in succession ἐφύλαξας ἔλυσας ἐξαποστελεῖς)[1] are there used in the same way with ὠδῖνας, the meaning being clear in no case; there can thus be no question of a phrase becoming current. Luke had before him the

---

[1] The second and third of these are variant renderings of תשלחנה in vs. 3.

words שרא חבליא די מותא, "loosing the bands of death." The quotation from Ps. was obvious, and he followed the LXX, as usual. The שרא he of course rendered literally.

2, 33. We do not speak of "pouring out" a miracle, but rather of "performing" it. We may suppose that the Aramaic was שפכה היא די אנתון חזיתון ולשמעתון, the formal equivalent of our Greek, but differently intended. The feminine suffix joined to the verb did not refer to the following, as it might naturally appear to, but to the word "spirit" (רוּחַ, πνεύματος) just preceding. The writer is returning to the prophecy of Joel, quoted in vs. 17. The translation should have been: "hath poured *it* out, *as* ye have seen and heard." [1]

3, 20 f. The plural in καιροί and χρόνων indicates duration, as in the original Aramaic. ἀπὸ προσώπου is presumably מִן קֳדָם, wherever it occurs. In this case it is merely "from," equivalent to Hebrew מֵאֵת. ἀποκατάστασις should mean here "establishment" in the sense of "*fulfilment*." ἀποκαθίστημι is used in Job 8, 6 to render שׁלם, a verb which would not be out of place in this passage. But the translation here is probably still closer; the verb rendered was in all likelihood a form (presumably the *haf'el*) of קוּם, cf. Dan. 9, 12 וַיָּקֶם אֶת דבריו אשר דבר עלינו, "and he *established* his words, which he spoke against us." This is exactly what the present passage requires, since it is speaking of the fulfilment of prophecy. We may suppose that the Aramaic was: עַד עִדָּנֵי הֲקָמוּת כֹּלָּא דִּי מַלֵּל אֱלָהָא וכו׳. This הקמות certainly meant "fulfilment"; but as it is a word capable of the meaning "restoration" in this context,[2] Luke rendered, as in other similar cases, by a Greek word which came as near as possible to leaving both interpretations open, while *agreeing in etymology* with the Aramaic original. This is perhaps as characteristic an example of his cautious exactitude as could be found.

3, 24. Καὶ πάντες δὲ οἱ προφῆται ἀπὸ Σαμουὴλ καὶ τῶν καθεξῆς ὅσοι ἐλάλησαν καὶ κατήγγειλαν τὰς ἡμέρας ταύτας. This can hardly pass as Greek. The καί before κατήγγειλαν is redundant; the phrase

---

[1] For Aramaic " that which," equivalent to " as," καθό, etc., cf. the note on 4, 22 ff., above.

[2] It should be observed that this *af'el* in the northern (Syriac) dialect is very often thus used. Notice, for example, how in the Syriac Hex. it renders ἀποκαθίστημι in 1 Esdr. 5, 2; Job 33, 25; Is. 1, 26 (Sym., Theod.); Am. 5, 15 (Aq., Sym., Theod.).

ἀπὸ . . . καθεξῆς is not idiomatic. Turned word for word into Aramaic it reads: וְכָל נְבִיָּא מִן שְׁמוּאֵל וְדִי בָתְרֵהּ דִּי מַלֵּלוּ וְהַכְרִיזוּ יוֹמַיָּא הָאִלֵּין.
"and all the prophets who spoke, from Samuel onward through his successors, announced these days." The Aramaic is entirely idiomatic; even the conjunction in וְהַכְרִיזוּ is not strange in Jewish Aramaic, introducing the apodosis in the Hebrew manner. It is perhaps worthy of notice, however, that this ו might very easily be a dittograph from the preceding, seeing that the two juxtaposed verbs would appear to be coördinate.

4, 12. Δεδομένον ἐν ἀνθρώποις is too literal. The Aramaic was יְהִיב בִּבְנֵי אֲנָשָׁא, "*put* among men"; יהב is very often the equivalent of שׂים, in all the Aramaic dialects, and is most commonly construed with ב. Characteristic examples are: "I *put* my bow in the cloud," Gen. 9, 13, Targ. Onkelos, Pesh.; "The royal crown which is *put* on (ב) his head," Esth. 6, 8, both Targums; "He found that he had been (*put*) in the tomb (יהיב ב׳) four days already," John 11, 17, Palest. Syr.; "[These things] they *put* in the midst of this sanctuary," Nabataean inscription from Puteoli (Cooke, *N. Sem. Inscrs.*, p. 256).[1] In Old Testament usage, God "puts" his name in one place or another.

The article τό is put before the word δεδομένον in this clause just in order to preserve the Aramaic order of words, and at the same time to separate δεδομένον from οὐρανόν!

4, 16. Γνωστόν is Aramaic ידיע, "notable, remarkable," which is what the context requires. "Manifest" will not do at all, in view of φανερόν at the end of the clause.

4, 36. Μεθερμηνευόμενον means, I think, "interpreted *euphemistically*." The very fact that a name is interpreted without apparent reason might lead us to suspect that something is wrong with it. Bar-Nebo (Nebo was a שֵׁיד, devil) was not, for church historians, a desirable name for such a saint as this — unless by means of *interpretation* the reproach could be removed. That the interpretation was far-fetched made no difference; whoever heard it was freed from the possibility of future embarrassment because of the name.

---

[1] Cf. further Luke 12, 50, "Think ye that I came to put (δοῦναι) peace in the earth?" also 15, 22, "*Put* (δότε) a ring on (εἰς) his hand."

A somewhat similar case is 13, 6–8. Here the narrative introduces a certain " false prophet " and " sorcerer " whose name was Bar-Jesus (so the original and therefore, of necessity, the Greek translation). But at the next mention of the man, his name is " interpreted " (μεθερμηνεύεται) into 'Ελύμας.¹ This is merely a euphemistic substitution; there is no need to suppose — nor is it probable — that the Greek name which was selected stood in any sort of relation to the Semitic name. An unfortunate *nomen atque omen* was replaced by one that was harmless, that is all. From that time on, it was certain that the false prophet would be known as " *Elymas* the Sorcerer," not " Bar-*Jesus* the Sorcerer." We have abundant evidence of the strong aversion felt to such collocations, and the euphemistic substitution, called in late Hebrew and Jewish Aramaic כִּנּוּי (ἐπίκλησις), was a common thing.²

In both passages it seems plain that the " interpretation " belongs to the translator, not to the Aramaic document. Only because of Luke's fidelity to his original was the true name preserved in 13, 6.

5, 7. This would be, in Aramaic: וַהֲוָה כִּתְלָת שָׁעִין וְעַלַּת אִנְתְּתֵהּ וכו'. The rendering is typical translation-Greek, as exact as it could be made. The διάστημα is presumably Luke's own, but it is implied in the Aramaic, which is precisely: " and there was the likeness (as to space) of three hours, and his wife entered," etc. Cf. Luke 5, 1, 12; 9, 28; 22, 59.

5, 13. Οὐδεὶς ἐτόλμα κολλᾶσθαι αὐτοῖς, " no one dared *join himself to* them," is immediately and flatly contradicted by vs. 14, " more were added to them, . . . multitudes both of men and women "! It is plain that we have here a mistranslation; what the writer must have intended to say is: " no one dared to *contend with*

---

¹ The attempt, made by many scholars, to connect the reading of D, Ετοιμας, with the Ἄτομον (?) of Jos., *Antt.* xx, 7, 2 seems to me mistaken for several reasons. Copyists very often miswrite λ as τ, and *vice versa*; while as for the replacing of υ by οι, so frequent in Greek MSS., Codex D is even capable of writing μὴ καὶ σοὶ ἐκ τῆς Γαλιλαίας εἶ; in John 7, 52! D therefore gives us no real variant here. The reading of Niese's edition is pretty certainly wrong, moreover, since σιμον and ατμον are practically identical in old Greek cursive script, and Simon is by far the more probable name.

² Observe that in the Peshitta version the name Bar-*Jesus* was not even permitted to stand in vs. 6, but Bar-*Shuma* was substituted for it!

them." More than one Aramaic root could supply forms capable of both of these meanings; קרב, for example, is a very good possibility. In Syriac, the *ethpa'al* might have either meaning. The Hebrew *hif'il* means "join"; the corresponding Syriac stem means "contend." Perhaps even more likely is לחם. The phrase would then have been לְהִתְלַחָמָה עַמְּהוֹן, the infinitive being used exactly as is the same form in late Hebrew, הִתְלַחֵם, "contend." But in the northern (Syrian) dialect the words would have meant "to be united with them"; cf. the passage cited in Payne Smith: בְּחַד עַמָּא אֶתְלַחַמוּ, "they were united into one people," and the root-meaning (*ibid.*) of לחם, *consociavit*.

5, 17. Preuschen: "ἀναστάς ist im Zusammenhang unmöglich." Wellhausen, *Analyse*, 10: "ἀναστάς ist sachlich unmöglich. Man erhebt sich um zu reden oder irgend etwas anderes zu tun, aber nicht um voll Leidenschaft zu werden. Glänzend hat Blass das sinnlose Wort in Ἄννας verbessert." See also his *Noten*, p. 21. Blass had proposed this emendation, introducing the name of the High Priest Annas, in the *Studien u. Kritiken*, 1896, p. 459. But the text is right as it stands; it is merely the omnipresent קָם, which is hardly more than "thereupon, straightway," used in much the same way as the unnecessary שָׁרֵי, ἤρξατο.[1] It does not represent action antecedent in time to that of the following verb, the two are rather coincident: "Then they started up, full of zeal, and laid their hands on the apostles." The insertion of a parenthetical (circumstantial) clause, וַהֲווֹ מְלַן קִנְאָה, literally "and they were filled with zeal," would be entirely idiomatic; compare e.g. Margolis, *Aramaic Language of the Babylonian Talmud*, § 69, *b*: בפניא אתא עניא והוה טריד כולי עלמא וליכא דשמעיה, "in the evening a poor man came, while everyone was busy, and there was none to hear him," etc. Such a clause would have been rendered here in just the words which we have, ἐπλήσθησαν ζήλου, the קָם having been translated by the participle, as usual in such cases.

5, 17. Πάντες οἱ σὺν αὐτῷ, ἡ οὖσα αἵρεσις τῶν Σαδδουκαίων. Wendt: "Das Part. ἡ οὖσα, statt οἱ ὄντες, ist attrahiert vom Prädikat." I believe he is mistaken in this. In the two passages

[1] See for example Dalman, *Worte Jesu*, 18 f.

(5, 17 and 13, 1) where this construction occurs it is merely Luke's careful way of reproducing the Aramaic אִית (the word אִית is exactly οὐσία). The phrase was this: דִּי אִיתַיהּ חֲבוּרְתָּא דִּי צַדּוּקָאֵי, "who were the sect of the Sadducees." See the note on 13, 1.

5, 28. The infinitive absolute, as idiomatic in Aramaic as in Hebrew.[1] The outwardly similar construction found in 23, 14 and 28, 10 (concrete nouns) is essentially different.

7, 38. Is it not likely that מִלֵּי חַיִּין, "*words of life*," was accidentally miswritten מִלִּין חַיִּין (מִלִּן חַיִּן), "living words"? Or is it merely the rendering that is at fault? The reference is plainly to such passages as Ezek. 20, 10 f.: "I brought them out of the land of Egypt, and into the wilderness; and I gave them my statutes and showed them my judgements, which if a man do, *he shall live by them*." Also Ezek. 33, 15; Lev. 18, 5; Deut. 30, 15-19, etc.

7, 52. Preuschen: "Der Ausdruck τοῦ δικαίου für den Messias wäre Juden kaum verständlich gewesen." This statement, unless hastily made, shows a very imperfect acquaintance with the Jewish conception of the Messiah. His chief office was to establish *justice* in the earth, Is. 42, 3 f.; cf. also 53, 11, etc., and the 17th and 18th of the Psalms of Solomon. See also the various designations of the Coming One as "the *righteous* Messiah" (Dalman, *Worte Jesu*, 240 f.).

7, 53. The curious phrase, "*unto ordinances of angels*," εἰς διαταγὰς ἀγγέλων. The εἰς represents לְ, meaning "according to," or "by." "Ye who received the Law לְפוּקְדָּנֵי מַלְאָכִין, by the ordering, or administration, of angels." For the use of the preposition compare for example Ps. 119, 91, לְמִשְׁפָּטֶיךָ, "according to thine ordinances"; 119, 154, לְאִמְרָתְךָ, "according to thy word," and many others. Luke's rendering here is not merely too literal, it is incorrect.

8, 7. The grammatical difficulty of the first clause is sufficiently familiar. Preuschen remarks that the text is "unheilbar verdorben"; see his commentary and that of Wendt for the catalogue of attempts, ancient and modern, to improve the reading; notice also the [παρὰ] πολλοῖς of Codex Bezae. In Aramaic, however, the suspended construction is not unusual, the anacoluthon being avoided

---

[1] Dalman, *Worte Jesu*, 27 f., exaggerates its rarity.

by the introduction of a suffixed pronoun in the latter part of the clause. For example: די סגיין מן אלין די אחרין הוו שידין מנהון צוחין בקל רב נפקו. This would almost inevitably be rendered into Greek by the exact form of words which we have before us. The translator would gain nothing, but only make his Greek worse, by rendering מנהון. His version was not in the least ambiguous, it was merely translation-Greek.

9, 2. "Any belonging to *the Way*." A genuine Semitic locution, which seems to have been taken over by the Gentile Christians from the speech of their Jewish brethren. Thus Talm. *Rosh Hashana* 17a, פִּירְשׁוּ מִדַּרְכֵי הַצִּבּוּר, "they separated themselves from the ways (religion) of the congregation," i.e., they became heretics. So also in old Syriac: *ūrḥā d'Ṭaiyāyūthā*, "the religion (literally *way*) of the Arabs"; *ūrḥā damshīḥā*, "the Christian religion"; other examples in Payne Smith, *Thesaurus*. So too in Arabic, *as-sabīl*, "the way," is used, without any further description or qualification, for the true (Mohammedan) religion. The adopted Gentile use in 19, 9, 23, etc.

9, 31*b*. This is probably the idiom which is so common in the Old Testament: Hebrew הלך ורב, Aramaic אָזֵל וְסָנֵא, "constantly increased," "abounded more and more," and the like. 1 Sam. 14, 19, "The tumult kept growing greater and greater" (πορευόμενος ... ἐπλήθυνεν); 2 Sam. 3, 1, "David grew stronger and stronger (ἐπορεύετο καὶ ἐκραταιοῦτο), while the house of Saul grew weaker and weaker (ἐπορεύετο καὶ ἠσθένει); Gen. 8, 5, "The water constantly diminished (πορευόμενον ἠλαττονοῦτο); and a great many similar cases.

9, 32. Peter passed through "*the whole* (region)," διὰ πάντων, בְּכֹלָּא. כלא is often used thus absolutely, when the context makes the meaning evident. For a Judean writer, to whom Palestine was "*the* land" (cf. כל ארעא in 11, 28, discussed above), this was doubtless the usual expression in such a context.

10, 11; 11, 5. The unusual ἀρχή in these two passages is the rendering of the much more common Aramaic רֵישׁ, "extremity, corner," etc. The participle καθιέμενον might represent either the root שָׁלְשֵׁל or שָׁרְבֵּב.

10, 30. "*On* (ἀπὸ) the fourth day (i.e., three days ago), *at* (μέχρι) this hour." This is not a permissible idiom in Greek, where the words would necessarily mean "for four days up to this hour." It is perfectly good Semitic, however: מִן יוֹמָא רְבִיעָיָא עַד שַׁעֲתָא דָא; that is, "on the fourth day back, reckoning up to this same hour."

10, 36 f. Τὸν λόγον ὃν ἀπέστειλεν, κ.τ.λ. Reduced to Aramaic this would sound much better, since the suspended construction is usual in that language. It is possible, too, that the last clause of vs. 36 was originally intended quite differently.

If the Aramaic had been מִלְּתָא דִי שְׁלַח לִבְנֵי יִשְׂרָאֵל מְבַסַּר שְׁלָם בְּיַד יֵשׁוּעַ מְשִׁיחָא הוּא מָרֵא כֹלָּא, it certainly might have been understood as we have it in Luke's word-for-word rendering. But it could also be translated as follows: "As for the word *which the Lord of All*[1] sent to the children of Israel, proclaiming good tidings of peace through Jesus Christ: ye know that which took place in all Judea," etc. This is at all events faultless Aramaic idiom. In favor of it may also be said: (1) The title מרא כלא, κύριος πάντων, according to all Jewish usage belongs to the Lord of Hosts, the God of Israel; and such titles are not easily given a new application. The Syriac equivalent, *Mārē Kul*, is a standing designation of the One God. In Hebrew we have the titles "Ruler over All" (1 Chr. 29, 12, etc.), "Maker of All" (Jer. 10, 16; 51, 19), probably "Captain of All" (שַׂר הַכֹּל, Dan. 11, 2),[2] and "Lord of All the Earth" (Josh. 3, 11, etc.). In Aramaic we have also, as standing titles of Yahwè, "Lord of the Heavens" (Elephantine Papyri, Dan. 5, 23, etc.), "Lord of the World" (Targums, *passim*), "Lord of All the World" (Targ. Micah 4, 13), Lord of the Worlds," whence Arabic *Rabb al-'Alamīn*; cf. also Ps. 145, 13, Tobit 13, 6, 10, etc.[3] It is intrinsically improbable, then, that the title "Lord of All" would have been applied to Jesus in a Judean Aramaic document of the first century. (2) Again, it is to be observed that what is especially emphasized in this whole passage is the purpose of the all-powerful God. He is

---

[1] Literally, "*this* Lord of All"; see the note on 1, 5, above, and cf. Dan. 2, 32, etc. The use of such a demonstrative pronoun is common in the Judean dialect. Here, moreover, there is a very obvious reason for its use, since *in the preceding verse* it had been said that the God of Israel is also the God *of all nations*.

[2] שר inserted by conjecture after עיר; see *Journ. Am. Or. Soc.* 25 (1904), pp. 310 f.

[3] The "Lord of all" in Rom. 10, 12 is of course not a title, nor to be compared with the present passage.

the God *of all nations* (vss. 34, 35); this Jesus was anointed of God (38); God was with him (*ibid.*); God raised him up (40); his witnesses were chosen of God (41); and they testify that God ordained him (42). This purpose of emphasis would be naturally served by the position of the subject, "the Lord of All," at the end of its clause in vs. 36.

For the case of ἀρξάμενος in vs. 37, see above, on 1, 22. As for the τὸν λόγον ὃν ἀπέστειλεν, at the beginning of vs. 36, the noun is to be taken as the direct object of οἴδατε (vs. 37).

10, 40. Ἔδωκεν αὐτὸν ἐμφανῆ γενέσθαι, i.e., יְהָבֵהּ לְהִתְחֲזָיָה. The same idiom in 14, 3; cf. also 2, 27 (quoted from LXX), and the many examples in the Greek O.T. Well known as a Semitism; Blass *Gramm.*, § 69, 4.

11, 4. On ἀρξάμενος, see above, on 1, 1; 1, 22, etc.

11, 6. The combination κατενόουν καὶ εἶδον (after ἀτενίσας!) would be remarkable as a specimen of Greek style. But this, exactly, is a favorite Aramaic idiom, אֶסְתַּכְּלִית וַחֲזֵית. See, for example, the Targ. Eccles. 9, 11: אסתכלית וחזית (not in the Hebrew); Targ. Is. 42, 18: אסתכלו וחזו (not so in the Hebrew); cf. also Dan. 7, 8, etc.

11, 16. "I remembered the word *of the Lord*, how that *he* said, John indeed baptized with water," etc. This was written by the author of 1, 4, obviously, and brings incidental confirmation of my demonstration (see below, page 59) that the Aramaic document used by Luke begins at 1, 1*b*.

11, 21. Καὶ ἦν χεὶρ κυρίου μετ' αὐτῶν. This is another plain Semitism. Cf. Luke 1, 66, etc., as well as the many passages in the Greek O.T.

11, 22. "The word was heard into the ears of the church." No Greek writer would ever have perpetrated this — unless he had wished to create the impression that he was using a Semitic "source." Even then, he would doubtless have used the standing LXX phrase, ἐν τοῖς ὠσί.

12, 11. "Expectation" is too weak for this context, which speaks of that from which Peter was *delivered*. Προσδοκία rendered מַחְשַׁבְתָּא, which ordinarily means "thought, opinion, calculation," and the like. But the word is not infrequently used, in Hebrew, Aramaic, and Syriac, to mean "*plot, machination.*" Thus Esther 8, 3: Esther besought the king to bring to nought that which Haman "had *plotted* (חשב) against the Jews"; Jer. 18, 18: "They said, Come, let us *lay plots* against Jeremiah"; Ps. 52, 4: "Thou *plottest* mischief with thy tongue"; and many other passages, both in the Hebrew O.T. and in the Targums.[1] The "Zamzummim" of Deut. 2, 20, interpreted as "*plotters*" (Heb. זמם, "devise evil"), are called in the Targum חָשְׁבָּנִין. An example in Syriac is John of Ephesus 18, 19 (I, 17): "treacherous *plotting.*"

12, 20. Θυμομαχῶν is presumably חָרֵא. This meant, in the speech of Judea, "*angry*," literally "burning"; thus also in the Hebrew of the Old Testament. But in the North-Syrian dialect the verb, used chiefly in the reflexive stem, means "*contend* against, *strive* with." Luke's rendering is a model of exactness, but the Judean meaning, "angry," is the correct one here.

13, 1. The phrase, κατὰ τὴν οὖσαν ἐκκλησίαν, "in the church which is (or, was) there." This is another example of the translation of אִית; see the note on 5, 17, above. The Aramaic was probably simply (or אִיתַיהּ) בְּעֵדְתָּא דִּי אִית, no accompanying adverb being necessary, since it was made evident by the context. The commentators sometimes compare Rom. 13, 1, also Acts 28, 17, etc.; but these passages are not really parallel cases, since in them the participle, or its equivalent, is indispensable. Other passages in the Aramaic half of Acts where אִית seems to be rendered are 11, 22 and 14, 13.

13, 22. "He raised up for them David as their king (εἰς βασιλέα)," אֲקִים לְהוֹן דָּוִיד לְמֶלֶךְ.

13, 24. This is altogether too literal a translation of מִן קֳדָם מֵיתוֹהִי, "before his coming." See the note on 3, 20, above.

13, 25. "As John was ending (literally, *fulfilling*) his course." Ἐπλήρου is the translation of Aramaic שְׁלִם; cf. the note on 2, 1, above.

13, 25. "*Who* do ye suppose that I am?" τί ἐμὲ ὑπονοεῖτε εἶναι; It can hardly be questioned that τί, rather than τίνα, has the presumption in its favor as the original reading. The fact that the

---

[1] The word ἐπίνοια in 8, 22 probably renders this same Aramaic word. Apparently there also the translation is too colorless.

neuter pronoun is "nicht erträglich" (Blass, in Wendt, p. 210) makes the case all the more interesting. This is the regular Aramaic idiom. No better illustration could be asked than that which is furnished by the Lewis[1] and Cur. Syriac renderings of Matt. 16, 13; Mk. 8, 27; Lk. 9, 18: "*Who* do men say that I am?" using only *mānā* ("what?"), in spite of the τίνα in every passage.

13, 25. Οὐκ εἰμὶ ἐγώ, "I am not *he*." It is worthy of note that the Aramaic (not Hebrew) idiom simply repeats the pronoun of the first person; "I am he" is אנא אנא. Thus e.g. the Syriac in John 4, 26: "I that speak with thee am *I*."

14, 17. There is apparently a mistranslation of some sort here. It is no more agreeable to usage in Aramaic or Greek to speak of 'filling hearts with food' than it is in English. Perhaps originally "Filling your hearts *with all* gladness" (cf. Rom. 15, 13); and confusion of מִכַּל with מֵאֲכַל "food," since the *nun* of the preposition was frequently assimilated at this time *in Judea, but very rarely elsewhere*. The verb מלא might of course be construed either with מִן or with direct object.

14, 27; 15, 4. The phrase ὅσα ἐποίησεν ὁ θεὸς μετ' αὐτῶν. On the difference of opinion among scholars as to the meaning of this, see Thayer, *Lexicon*, s. v. μετά. It is, however, merely translation-Greek, meaning: "what God had done *to* (or *for*) them." There is no idea of coöperation in the phrase, nor even of accompaniment. This is the regular idiom in all branches of Aramaic. Thus, an inscription from Tarsus, fifth century B.C. (*Journ. Am. Or. Soc.* 35, Part 4): "Whoever *does* (יעבד) any harm *to* (עם) this image," etc. Dan. 3, 32: "the wonders which God *has wrought upon me*" (עבד עמי). Assemani, *Bibl. Or.* III, ii, 486: "the miracle which was *performed on* their king" (מתעבד עם מלכהן). The idiom is also found in Hebrew; see Deut. 1, 30; 10, 21, etc.

15, 16-18. Luke always uses the Greek Bible for his Old Testament quotations; see my *Aramaic Gospels*, 298 ff. In this case, we do not know to what extent the Greek varied from the Aramaic — or rather, Hebrew—which actually lay before him. Rabbi Akiba and his fellows had not yet set up a "standard" text of the Prophets; the

---

[1] The Lewis Syriac in Matt. 16, 13 follows a different text, to be sure.

author of this Aramaic document was at liberty to select the reading which best suited his purpose; and the LXX rendering of Am. 9, 11 f. certainly represented a varying *Hebrew* text. But even our Massoretic Hebrew would have served the present purpose admirably, since it predicted that "the tabernacle of David," i.e. the church of the Messiah, would "gain possession of all the nations which are called by the name [of the God of Israel]." Cf. vs. 14, where we are told what this quotation was expected to prove: ὁ θεὸς ἐπεσκέψατο λαβεῖν ἐξ ἐθνῶν λαὸν τῷ ὀνόματι αὐτοῦ.

As for the troublesome ending of vs. 18, I believe that the explanation is this: Instead of עֹשֶׂה זֹאת, as in the Massor. Hebrew, the reading of our document was מוֹדִיעַ זֹאת מֵעוֹלָם — a very natural improvement; cf. especially the ἀφ' ἡμερῶν ἀρχαίων in vs. 7. Luke, in giving the quotation in Greek, wrote out his LXX word for word, as usual. Arriving at the end of the verse, instead of rendering מוֹדִיעַ by γνωρίζων he was able, by the periphrasis ποιῶν ταῦτα γνωστά, "*making these things known*," to be faithful both to his Greek Bible (ποιῶν ταῦτα) and to the document which he was translating. This is thoroughly characteristic of Luke; cf. for example the notes on 2, 1 and 2, 24, above.

15, 23. Harnack, *Lukas der Arzt*, 154, speaks of the "merkwürdige Ausdruck οἱ πρεσβύτεροι ἀδελφοί," and Preuschen, *Komm.*, declares this beginning of the address "unerträglich." But it is faultless Aramaic idiom. In the phrase שְׁלִיחַיָּא וְקַשִּׁישַׁיָּא אַחַיָּא, the word "brethren" would naturally refer to *both* the nouns preceding; if it had been intended to refer to the "elders" alone, it would have stood between this word and the conjunction ו. From the Christian Aramaic (Syriac) which we know, it is evident that in early church usage this apposed "brethren" was very common.

15, 28. Πλὴν τούτων τῶν ἐπάναγκες. Professor G. F. Moore has suggested (orally) what seems to me the correct explanation of this improbable phrase. The Greek originally read: ἔδοξεν ... μηδὲν πλέον ἐπιτίθεσθαι ὑμῖν βάρος πλὴν τούτων· ἐπάναγκες ἀπέχεσθαι κ.τ.ἑ., the τῶν being due to dittography.[1] ἐπάναγκες ἀπέχεσθαι ren-

[1] Clem. Alex. seems to have read in just this way in his *Stromata* iv, 16, 97; this reading of his was probably obtained merely by accident or conjecture, however.

ders צְרִיךְ לְאִתְרְחָקָה, which according to Moore was probably the reading of the Aramaic document in this passage.

The translation-Greek continues to the end of 15, 35, which probably formed the original conclusion of the Aramaic narrative (see below).[1] With verse 36 the character of the language changes completely, so far as its structure is concerned, and the Aramaic idiom does not appear again, even for a single paragraph. Two other facts deserve especial attention. The first is, that the author of the Greek half of the book *composed his narrative as the continuation of the Aramaic document.* This is sufficiently obvious, not only from the way in which vs. 36 takes its start from vs. 35, but also from the correspondence of the details of the narrative in 15, 36–16, 5 with those in the chapters immediately preceding; a relationship much too close to be accidental. The allusions to the churches already established in Asia are plainly intended as the sequel of chapters 13 and 14; 16, 4 is only comprehensible after reading 15, 1–29; 15, 38 refers to 13, 13; the speech of Paul in 17, 22–31 seems to be modeled on that in 14, 15–17, though the resemblance may be merely accidental (see below); and there are other striking correspondences. This is of course just what we should expect in view of the remarkable uniformity of vocabulary and phraseology in all parts of the book, showing (as already noted above) that the translator of the first half was the author of the second. The other fact deserving notice is this, that the author, translator, and compiler was *a man singularly faithful to his sources.* He disliked to alter, even slightly, the document in his hands, even where he believed its statements to be mistaken, and where he found himself obliged to contradict them. Acts 1, 3 (the "forty days"), for instance, is flatly opposed to the statements in Luke 24 (see below), and the statement in Acts 1, 4 ("which ye heard from me") was certainly recognized as erroneous by the author of Luke 3, 16. As we have seen, the name of the sorcerer Bar-Jesus was allowed to stand in 13, 6, though the

[1] Attention may be called at this point to the evidence furnished by the foregoing investigation that the *text* of Acts which has come down to us, especially in Cod. B and its nearest associates, is very old and correct. The later and all but worthless text of Cod. Bezae and its associates I hope to make the subject of a future study.

substitute "Elymas" was used thereafter. The many cases of very faithful translation noted above, in passages where a somewhat freer rendering would have saved the translator from real difficulties, are in the same line of evidence. But perhaps the most striking illustration of the kind is afforded by the point where the transition is made from the Aramaic history to Luke's own narrative. Luke did not believe that Silas returned to Jerusalem as narrated in 15, 33, but rather (see vss. 36 and 40), that he remained at Antioch until the time when he set out with Paul on the missionary journey. It would have been easy to omit vs. 33, or to add a harmonizing statement, as some less scrupulous editor of the text has actually done in the vs. 34 which is now omitted from all critical editions. But Luke, as usual, gave his source the word, and would not falsify it.[1]

[1] I mean, of course, that this was his way of dealing with a unique document of great importance *which he was translating*. No one will doubt that he was quite ready to edit, to omit, and to supplement with his own freely composed material, wherever these activities were in place. He may have made numerous slight editorial additions here, though this does not seem to me a necessary supposition, and I do not believe that it would be possible to recognize them. Professor J. H. Ropes has given me the very plausible suggestion, for instance, that the list of the apostles in 1, 13 is Luke's own addition, since it so closely resembles his list in Lk. 6, 14 f. But the Aramaic document can hardly have been without such a list at this point, in view of the episode which follows. Moreover, Luke's own list was certainly derived from a Semitic source.

# CHAPTER II

## THE INTEGRITY OF THE SECOND HALF OF ACTS

### § 1. The Homogeneity of II Acts

It is beyond controversy that *the general impression* made by the second half of the Book of Acts is one of homogeneity. Phraseology, literary style, point of view of the writer, and mode of treatment of the material, are noticeably the same throughout chapters 16–28; it would be quite futile for any one to attempt to demonstrate the contrary, in any of these particulars. Nevertheless the unity of this half of Acts has long been called in question, perhaps by a majority of the best scholars, and for reasons which are obvious.[1] The book of Acts as a whole is plainly composite; the "Hebraizing" character of the opening chapters, in contrast with the smooth Greek of the last chapters, has long been the subject of comment. It is the style of these opening chapters that most resembles that of the Third Gospel; and the introductory words, mentioning Theophilus and referring to the "former treatise," are inseparably welded to the following history (see below). The Christology of the early chapters, moreover, could not easily be attributed to a Gentile companion of Paul. No theory of *translation* of documents has seemed to give any help (especially as it has always been taken for granted that the sources of the Third Gospel were Greek sources), nor has there seemed to be any way of establishing such a theory. Then was added the riddle of the "We-sections," giving such an inviting opportunity for theories of composition. Furthermore, Acts 15 was felt to be in disagreement with Gal. 2, so much so that it was hardly conceivable that Paul's travelling companion could have written it. Yet Acts 15 could not be separated from chapters 13 f. and 16, 1–5.

---

[1] In the sequel, "I Acts" is used for chaps. 1, 1–15, 35, and "II Acts" for 15, 36–28, 31.

Hence also, apparently, the necessity of separating the "travel-document" from the preceding account. The fact that portions of the narrative are plainly untrustworthy as a record of events, while other portions are as evidently historical, also seemed to some to give a starting point for theories of composite authorship. Finally, the supposed necessity of postulating a late date for the entire work — the Third Gospel being later than Mark and Matthew, and Acts later than the Gospel — gave support to the view that at least the "travel-document" of II Acts was an older source incorporated in the main work. After a beginning of analysis had thus been made, there was no obvious halting place; it was simply a question of who should be most ingenious and plausible in discovering joints, alterations, and redactional patches.

The "We-sections" — to begin with these — present no difficulty when the fact of Luke's translation of the Aramaic document is recognized. The reason for the employment of the first person is merely this, that the author of the account himself took part in some of the events which are described, and was historian enough to feel the importance of indicating the fact, though he does it in a very modest way. In the portions of the narrative in which the third person is used, in contexts where we should have expected the author to indicate his participation if he had really been present, it is most natural to suppose that he was not himself a participant in the events, but obtained his information from others. Eduard Norden, *Agnostos Theos*, 317–324, shows that the contemporary literature, both Greek and Roman, contains numerous exact parallels to II Acts in this regard, and that if more of the writings of the time had been preserved we should doubtless have had many other examples. The demonstration is unnecessary, to be sure, since this has always and everywhere been the most natural way of composing an unpretentious and *bona fide* narrative of events partially witnessed by the writer; and it is such a narrative which we have before us.

The point at which Luke's use of the first person begins, 16, 10, seems to make it plain that he joined Paul's company at Troas; and we know from vss. 12–17 that he went on with the others to Philippi and remained there with them. In the events narrated in vss. 18–39 Luke of course took no part, and the first person therefore could not have been used by him. When we read " the brethren," rather than " us," in vs. 40, it is possible to conclude that Paul and Silas left Philippi without seeing Luke after their release from prison; but it is quite as likely that his modesty (so abundantly attested) is the true reason for his failure to include himself expressly. In 17, 1–20, 4 the total absence of the first person, where it might reasonably be expected from the usage elsewhere in the document, is noticeable; and it can hardly be accidental that it is on the return of Paul and his party to Philippi that the author's " we " begins again to be employed, in 20, 5 f. It is safe to conclude that Luke did not go with the others through Macedonia and Greece, and through the other journeyings described in 17, 1–20, 5, but remained in Philippi. This part of his account he composed on the basis of oral information obtained from his friends.[1] From this time on, however, he seems always to have been a member of Paul's party, whenever the apostle was accompanied by a group of his helpers. There was of course no opportunity or excuse for using the first person plural in 20, 17–38. The same is true in 21, 19–26, 32, the account of the imprisonment and trial of Paul;[2] only a writer with an undue sense of his own importance would have intruded himself here, where he played no part in the events narrated.[3] In 27, 1–28, 15 Luke had the opportunity to tell in some detail the story of the journey to Italy, and especially of the shipwreck; a series of happenings of which he remembered (naturally enough!) many striking incidents. Phraseology and literary style, as well as the close connection with

[1] Judging from the scale on which the history is written where Luke was an eye-witness, he would have given us very much more than this meager sketch of a few pages (covering seven or eight years, at least, and including by far the most important parts of the great missionary journeys!) if he had had personal knowledge of the events. His information seems in fact to have been scanty and incidental.

[2] Literary criticism more thoroughly unscientific than some of the current " analysis " of II Acts on the basis of the occurrence of the first person plural, it would be hard to find. See, for example, Wellhausen's *Kritische Analyse*, p. 34.

[3] In 24, 23 (end) we may have a hint of the historian's presence. Compare what was said above in regard to 16, 40.

## THE INTEGRITY OF THE SECOND HALF OF ACTS 45

what has preceded, show plainly enough that the same writer is composing the narrative.[1]

### § 2. THE THEORIES OF NORDEN AND OTHERS

A typical specimen of the attempts to find interpolations in the original account is afforded by certain comments on the passage 27, 9–11. Wellhausen, *Noten zur A G*, 17, says of these verses: "Es braucht nicht noch bewiesen zu werden, dass der Vers 12 hinter V. 9–11 gar nicht zu verstehen ist, sondern unmittelbar an V. 8 anschliesst. Der Passus V. 9–11 ist mithin eine Einlage von zweiter Hand." But by what process of divination is this conclusion reached? for it is only by divination, not through any scientific process, that the thing can be done. How is it possible for any one to know that the words of the passage do not mean what they appear to mean? The party arrives at Καλοὶ Λιμένες, in Crete; Paul advises them to stay there, saying that if they proceed further (as they obviously intend) they will suffer loss; the officers do not heed his words, but since the harbor was not fit for wintering, decide to put to sea in the hope of reaching Phoenix. There is no semblance of incongruity here, unless one taxes his ingenuity to create it. And cannot the main course of a narrative be interrupted by an episode without arousing the suspicion of an interpolation? Wendland, *Die hellenistisch-römische Kultur*[2], 324, after giving the substance of verses 8, 12, and 13, proceeds: "Dazwischengeschoben ist eine Warnung des Paulus vor Fortsetzung der Fahrt, *obgleich diese ja gar nicht beabsichtigt war*" (the italics are mine). If the wording of the narrative makes any one thing evident, it is this, that at no time did those in charge of the vessel have any other intention than that of a

---

[1] Wellhausen, *Krit. Analyse*, 34, remarks: "Und ferner zeigen die beiden grossen Partien, in denen das Wir sich wirklich zeigt, eine erheblich verschiedene Art, so dass es recht zweifelhaft wird, ob in 20, 6–21, 16 der selbe Erzähler rede wie in Kap. 27." This is an assertion which neither Wellhausen nor any one else could substantiate. The *subject matter* is "erheblich verschieden," and the manner of the narrative is affected accordingly; but this is all. As for the nautical knowledge displayed in chap. 27, one can only say that a man who could have spent as many long months on the sea, in many ships, as this writer, without learning at least this much, must have been unusually stupid.

"Fortsetzung der Fahrt." Verses 7 f. show that they put in at Fair Havens not because they wished to stop there, but because of the unabating fury of the wind. Vs. 9a (ἱκανοῦ δὲ χρόνου διαγενομένου) makes it plain that they were anxious to depart, but were still hindered for a considerable time by the wind, and vs. 12 (εἴ πως δύναιντο) shows the same. Of course the pilot and the shipmaster did not need ἱκανόν χρόνον in order to ascertain that the harbor was not fit for wintering; the first glance would have shown it, even if they had not known it all their lives. Only a very strong desire to solve the problems believed to be present in II Acts could account for the perverse criticism of this passage. See also *Agnostos Theos*, 314 Anm. 1, and Preuschen's *Apostelgeschichte*. The objections raised against 27, 21–26 (see e.g. Wendt, 355 f.) are equally futile and hardly more plausible; and there are other similar cases.[1]

The speech of Paul at Athens, recorded in chapter 17, has recently been subjected to very searching criticism by Norden in his *Agnostos Theos*. I have read the book with great enjoyment, finding it immensely interesting and stimulating; I am unable to see, however, that it throws any light on the *composition* of the Book of Acts.

[1] Certainly some of the attempted dissection of the Book of Acts is due to misunderstanding of the mental attitude and predispositions of the narrator, and of the readers for whom he wrote. The attempt to find, in either I Acts or II Acts, at least *one* writer who thought and narrated after the manner of a modern historian is doomed to failure. To all such as could possibly have composed these histories, or any part of them, there was one and the same persuasion in regard to the aid given by God to his chosen emissaries through visions, dreams, angels, and manifestations of supernatural power. These things were not only a matter of course, they were also a necessity. Paul was a prophet (26, 16 ff.), and being such, had the power of foreseeing future events (universally recognized as the principal characteristic of the Hebrew prophets) as well as of working miracles. If he had not possessed these powers, he would not have been worthy of credence. Luke does not profess to have seen or heard any of these marvellous happenings himself; they were reported by villagers and boatmen, who knew that a prophet was travelling among them, and neither Luke nor any of his fellows could have doubted their truth for an instant. The only remarkable thing is that they are so few in number. Those who think that considerable time is needed for the growth and wide acceptance of such legends, or that their adoption by an early Christian historian shows him to have been of an especially credulous turn of mind, should read the life of St. Simeon Stylites written during his own lifetime by the cultivated and truth-loving scholar Theodoret (*Historia religiosa* xxvi), who was a near neighbor and personal friend of the great ascetic.

Norden attempts to show, first, that the speech in 17, 22-31 conforms to the recognized model of a missionary sermon; he succeeds, however, only in demonstrating what was already known. It is true that the religious propagandist was a long-familiar figure at that time; also true that many of these missionary preachers were men of wide learning and broad sympathy (it was for this very reason, generally speaking, that they had seen new light and wished to share it); and a matter of course, finally, that the speaker or writer fashioned his discourse according to his purpose. It was of the highest importance to set forth in a worthy and attractive manner — though in brief compass — the nature of God and of his relation to man, and the spiritual character of his worship. Cultivated Hellenistic Jews and cultivated Greeks would have had very much the same message to give, in these regards, in the first century. The polemic against idolatry, too, was of course always familiar. It was manifestly important also to be conciliatory, especially when it came to rebuking or correcting the accepted beliefs and practices. Even a tyro would recognize the wisdom of commending whatever could be commended in the religion or religious history of his hearers. Mohammed, for instance, unites all these elements, even the conciliatory, in his exhortations in the Koran. These things could all be taken for granted. But the question of a commonly-used *literary* scheme of the missionary discourse, as distinct from other discourses ("Dass der Verfasser der Areopagrede sich an ein ihm überliefertes Schema anschloss," *Agnostos Theos*, 3), is quite another matter. The existence of such a scheme is intrinsically improbable, and the specimens cited by Norden certainly do not give the idea any new plausibility. His "parallel" columns, pp. 6 f., show only the vaguest resemblances on the lines indicated above: *knowledge of God; nature of true worship; need of turning from the old way to the new; promise of a blessed future.* These are merely the essentials of any religion, and consequently of any religious propaganda. Even the logical order is obvious. Thus, we have in the Koran, 11, 52-55, a typical specimen of a brief missionary sermon. The prophet Hūd is sent to the 'Adites and preaches to them in the following words: "O my people! Worship (εὐσεβεῖτε) God; ye have no god but Him (ἐποίησε πᾶν ἔθνος). Ye have only false knowledge (ἄγνοιαν). 53 I do not ask you for any reward; my reward rests with Him who created me (διδοὺς πᾶσι ζωήν). Will ye not have understanding (γνῶσιν)?[1] 54 Ask your Lord for forgiveness, and then turn to Him (μετανοήσατε). He will then send upon you rain in abundance, 55 and will add strength to your strength (τῶν αὐτοῦ ἀγαθῶν ἀπολαύσετε). Do not then sinfully turn your backs." Similarly Joseph preaches to his companions in prison (12, 37-40): 37, 'I have wisdom revealed to me from God. I turned from the false way to the right way, belief in God and in the world to come.' 38, Monotheism; a blessing from God. 39, Monotheism better than a plurality of gods. 40, The times of ignorance; lack of the true wisdom; the right worship. These examples are both nearer to Norden's "type" than some of those printed in his parallel columns.[2] Or, turning to the Old Testament, take the discourse of Wisdom in Prov. 1, 22-33: Need of wisdom (22); repentance (23); 24-32 are negative, describing the fate of fools; promise of blessing (33). Such examples could easily be multiplied. Norden's specimens are typical only in this same general way; of anything that could fairly be called a scheme of literary composition there is not a trace. And since even so widely read and keen-eyed an observer as he has not been able to demonstrate anything of the sort, it is not likely that another will succeed where he has failed.

Norden's attempt (pp. 13-24) to point out specifically Stoic elements in the speech at Athens is equally unsuccessful. These are all mere commonplaces in Jewish theology, whether Palestinian or Hellenistic. 'God has no need of anything that man can give' (Acts 17, 25); cf. Ps. 50, 12, precisely the same thing. 'Reaching after God and *touching* him' (27a); the figure of speech is not in any way remarkable, cf. Is. 64, 7, Job 19, 21, Jer. 1, 9, such passages

[1] Verse 51, introducing this account of Hûd, deals entirely with hidden *wisdom*, revealed by God to his prophets.

[2] Norden is mistaken (p. 7, note 1), in thinking that in Ode Sol. 33, 8, there is a reference to γνῶσις. It is simply the oft-repeated contrast between the *corrupt* way, vs. 7, and the *right* way (דרך הישרה), vs. 8. He is also hardly justified in claiming (p. 5) that the mention of the resurrection of Christ in his first and fourth columns is a substitute (!) for the promise of eternal life given in the others.

as Job 4, 15 f., 23, 3, 8, 9, and many others. 'He is not far from each one of us' (27b); cf. Deut. 4, 7, Ps. 145, 18.[1] 'In him we live, and move, and have our being' (28); cf. Job 12, 10, Dan. 5, 23, Wisd. 7, 16, Hebr. 2, 11. Neither the ideas nor the language of the speech, then, can be said to show the influence of the Stoa. Such ideas as these were older, and had far wider currency, than many have been wont to believe.

As for the altar "*to the unknown god*," Norden shows, as others had done before, that there was at that time at Athens an altar which was pretty widely known, bearing an inscription mentioning ἄγνωστοι θεοί, and that altars ἀγνώστων θεῶν were also to be seen in other places. Norden undertakes to prove that Apollonius of Tyana, on the occasion of his holding a διάλεξις in Athens, took as his starting point this altar of "unknown gods," interpreted its presence as a sign of unusual δεισιδαιμονία, and then urged that so god-fearing a city ought to receive the knowledge of the highest God, who is a spirit, has no need of any offering that men could bring, and ought not to be represented by images. This address of Apollonius at Athens was contained, according to Norden, in his treatise περὶ θυσιῶν, of which the only extant fragment hitherto recognized is quoted by Eusebius in the well-known passage derived from Porphyrius. Norden then draws the conclusion (p. 52) that we have before us a plain case of literary dependence, and that the author of the "Speech of Paul" is the borrower. If the validity of Norden's demonstration of the above details could be admitted, it would be difficult to escape from his conclusion. But when his argument is examined, it is seen to break down at every essential point.

The weight of the argument lies of course in the collocation of so many points of correspondence in the general situation, as well as in the more striking details. Norden names (p. 51) as the typical elements in the story told of both Paul and Apollonius the following: *visiting a city; noticing a remarkable inscription on an altar; making a religious discourse;* and *taking as the starting point of the*

---

[1] One can hardly believe his eyes when he reads Norden's words, p. 19, after quoting the passage from Dion: "Die Übereinstimmung der Worte καί γε οὐ μακράν = ἅτε γὰρ οὐ μακράν schliesst die Möglichkeit einer bloss zufälligen Berührung aus"!

*discourse the altar inscription.* This last-named element does not occur, to be sure, in any account of Apollonius. Norden thinks that it can be postulated for him, saying (*ibid.*): " denn da von den vier Komponenten, aus denen das Motiv sich zusammensetzt, . . die ersten drei für die athenische Rede des Apollonios überliefert sind, so muss auch der vierte, als der aus dem zweiten und dritten notwendig resultierende für ihn angenommen werden." As to this, there are two things to be said. *First*, the word " überliefert " is used here in a very misleading way. By " *the* speech of Apollonius at Athens " Norden means the (conjectured) address which he supposes to have been contained in the περὶ θυσιῶν, and which — unless his whole argument is to fall to the ground — contained (1) a protest against neglect and contempt of the gods and their worship (giving it a connection with the disputation mentioned on p. 38), and (2) an allusion to the altar ἀγνώστων δαιμόνων (giving it a connection with the conversation mentioned on p. 42). As for (1): Norden remarks, p. 43, that we know " aus der vorhin angeführten Inhaltsangabe " that this protest stood in the περὶ θυσιῶν. But how can this statement be justified? The portion of the "Inhaltsangabe " (p. 38) which mentions the protest of Apollonius concerns *only* his rebuke of the blaspheming Athenian hierophant. It is not said, nor even implied, that this rebuke stood in the περὶ θυσιῶν; on the contrary, the plain impression gained from the wording of the passage is, that this treatise (βιβλίον) had been published *before* Apollonius had this experience in Athens. To assume, as Norden does, that the publication had its origin in the διάλεξις held in that city, is gratuitous and absolutely unwarranted. As for (2), the allusion to the altar to " unknown gods ": the conversation (it is no formal discourse) in which this occurs is expressly said to have occurred *in Egypt*! Norden's statement, then, that the incident of noticing a remarkable inscription on an altar " für die athenische Rede des Apollonios *überliefert* ist," is an amazing perversion of the facts. This is not obtained from " tradition " of any sort, but only from an audacious combination of Norden's, which, as I shall show, cannot for a moment be allowed. *Secondly*, in regard to Norden's claim that if the first three of the " typical elements " above mentioned are admitted, the fourth follows of necessity. For a conclusive answer to this, it is only necessary to point to the passage quoted by him, p. 42, containing the mention of the altar. This very passage might conceivably have stood in the περὶ θυσιῶν (as Norden imagines that it did); and this casual, but effective, allusion to the Athenian altar [1] might perfectly well have been the *only* mention of it in the work. Why not? To demand more than this is merely to beg the question.

And now in regard to the way in which Norden contrives to transfer to Athens the conversation held by Apollonius in Egypt with the young man from Naukratis. The sage is pleased with his reverence of Aphrodite, and compliments him. The youth has had a painful domestic experience, similar to that of Hippolytus in the house of his father Theseus; and Apollonius is thus reminded of the hero, and led to contrast his impious treatment of Aphrodite with the piety of the young man. He declares that the latter is more worthy of reverence than the other, who spoke against the goddess in so ill-judged a manner; and adds, with pleasant irony: "More sensible to speak well of all gods (σωφρονέστερον γὰρ τὸ περὶ πάντων θεῶν εὖ λέγειν), *especially at Athens, where they even have altars to unknown divinities.*" Norden assumes that "to speak well of all gods" refers to the youth from Naukratis, and is much mystified by the sentence. Why in all the world, he asks (p. 42), should there be mention of *Athens* here? and he concludes, that the saying of Apollonius has been taken out of its original setting; it must have stood in a context the scene of which was Athens rather than the Nile. This hypothesis brings with it considerable difficulty, to be sure, as Norden remarks. The youth "hat sich gar nicht an den Göttern vergangen," nor has he spoken well of "all gods"; why then these pointless words in regard to him? We must also suppose an astonishing stupidity on the part of the author of the story (Philostratus) in not seeing this, and in permitting the senseless reference to Athens ("absurde Uebertragung," Norden, p. 44) to stand; especially since,

---

[1] Norden speaks of it (p. 42, below) as "das athenische Kultuskuriosum, *auf das die ganze Geschichte angelegt ist.*" Has this assertion any basis whatever, aside from Norden's own imagination?

as Norden himself declares, he had invented this whole story of Apollonius in Egypt, and could therefore have fashioned it. to suit himself. But the true solution is much simpler than the one proposed by Norden. It is this, that the problematic words were not spoken of the youth, to whom they do not seem to belong, but of Hippolytus, to whom in every way they do seem to belong. He was born at Athens, his father was king of that city, his tomb was shown there, and, according to many writers, Athens was the scene of the greater part of his life. Evidently Apollonius — or rather, Philostratus — was one of those who held this view.[1]

Thus disappears the last vestige of support for Norden's main contention. When, therefore, he claims (p. 44, below) to have shown not only that Apollonius made a speech at Athens in which he mentioned altars ἀγνώστων θεῶν, but also that " die Ubereinstimmung zwischen ihm und den Worten des Areopagredners erstreckt sich bis in die Nuance des Ausdruckes hinein," we can only reply, that nothing whatsoever tending to substantiate this remarkable assertion has thus far come to light. Until some new evidence is dis-

[1] Norden also wishes to claim for the περὶ θυσιῶν the words put by Philostratus into the mouth of Apollonius in the anecdote of the Egyptian temples, p. 41. He says: " Die ihm hier in den Mund gelegte Empfehlung eines bildlosen Gottesdienstes und einer entsprechenden Regelung des Opferrituals war wenigstens für den höchsten Gott durch die erwähnte Schrift [the π.θ.] beglaubigt." And again, p. 43: " Es kann nicht auf Zufall beruhen, dass wir vorhin auf die fiktive äthiopische Situation aus der realen athenischen bereits ein anderes Motiv, das der bildlosen Verehrung des höchsten Gottes, übertragen fanden: dieses Motiv ist für die athenische Rede durch das erhaltene Fragment aus der Schrift περὶ θυσιῶν bezeugt." That is, he claims two points of contact: (1) worship without images, and (2) a corresponding regulation of the sacrificial cult. But this is only another glaring example of too easy-going argumentation. Nothing whatever is said in the anecdote (as Norden asserts) about " einer entsprechenden Regelung des Opferrituals "; that appears *only* in the περὶ θυσιῶν, regarding the Highest God; nothing whatever is said in the extract from the περὶ θυσιῶν (as Norden asserts) in regard to " bildlose Verehrung des höchsten Gottes." We do not know that this work contained a single word about images of gods. The remarks of Apollonius (Philostratus) against the Egyptian images were called out (as Norden says, 41 line 6) by the fact that they gave their gods the forms of beasts and birds. Thus the " correspondence " said to be so close that it " kann nicht auf Zufall beruhen," turns out to be purely imaginary. Both of Norden's statements are unwarranted, and the argument is worthless.

covered we may fairly say, *exit Apollonius*, so far as Acts 17 is concerned.[1]

So far as language and style are concerned, there is no ground for differentiating the account of Paul at Athens, or any part of it, from the context in which it stands. Norden (333 ff.) points out certain words and phrases in vss. 18 and 21: σπερμολόγος, λέγειν ἢ ἀκούειν, and καινότερον, and shows that they are λέξεις 'Αττικαί. He then says in regard to them (p. 335): " Alles zusammengenommen, kann ich nicht glauben, dass der Redaktor der Acta, dessen Sprache doch wahrlich nichts Attisches an sich hat, diese Stelle ohne ein literarisches Vorbild komponiert haben könnte." But one cannot help feeling that the widely experienced and accomplished author of II Acts may himself have been familiar with λέξεις 'Αττικαί, perhaps even more than any modern scholar. There is a very obvious reason why he should have employed these locutions where we find them, and an equally obvious reason why he would *not* have employed Atticisms in the rest of his history; it would have been an absurd affectation, since they did not belong to the literary language which he, and Theophilus, and their circles, were accustomed to use.

There is nothing in the speech on the Areopagus that Paul himself *might* not have said. Our reasons for believing that the words are not his, but Luke's are: *first*, that the speech does not sound like Paul; and *secondly* (a very potent reason), our knowledge of the literary habit of ancient authors, in freely composing speeches, dialogues, letters, and other documents, for the embellishment of their histories. *All* the speeches and letters in I and II Acts are presumably free compositions of the authors of the two documents in which they stand.[2]

[1] It is a pity that a work of such learning as the *Agnostos Theos* should be so marred by inaccurate statements and loose reasoning, especially when the problem in hand is such an important one. It has seemed desirable to examine its argument here at some length, since so many scholars, including the most recent commentators on Acts (Wellhausen, *Krit. Anal.*, 36 note; Preuschen, *Apgesch.*, vi; Wendt, *Komm.*, Vorwort), have declared themselves convinced by it.

[2] This of course applies not only to such documents as 23, 26–30, but also to the letter of the Apostles, 15, 23–29, which was written in Aramaic. For a more extended discussion of this whole subject, especially as touching Jewish literature, the " documents " in Ezra-Neh., in I Maccabees, etc., I would refer to my *Ezra Studies*, pp. 145–150, 206, 245.

As for the change, which seems to have been made, from ἀγνώστοις θεοῖς to τῷ ἀγνώστῳ θεῷ, it is entirely harmless *as the introduction to a speech*. It is merely an orator's device, which has been in common use in all ages, the purpose being to catch and hold the close attention of the audience.[1] I heard precisely this thing done, with striking effect, a few years ago; the speaker beginning his address by referring to a picture (in reality notably different from his description of it) which he declared to be hanging in the building in which the address was delivered. No one was deceived, but all were captivated by the audacious irony of the orator. It is to be remembered also that Paul had been brought up in the strictest Jewish sect, and that the Jews, like the Mohammedans, had a strong dislike of even repeating words which imply a plurality of gods. There may thus have been also a mild protest here, in the substitution of the singular for the plural. See also Wendt's excellent remarks (p. 257), and Norden's demonstration of the fact that the singular number, ἄγνωστος θεός, was also familiar at that time, though not (so far as we know) as an inscription on any altar.

[1] It would have been a totally different matter, for instance, if Paul had been represented as writing a letter to his friends at home, saying that when he was in Athens he saw an altar inscribed " to the unknown god "!

# CHAPTER III

## THE RELATION OF II ACTS TO I ACTS

### § 1. Old Testament Quotations and Language in Acts

Interesting confirmation of the results thus far reached is afforded by a study of the manner of using the Old Testament in the two halves of the book. As has been observed, II Acts is almost entirely free from Semitisms, and shows no trace of the Aramaic idiom which is omnipresent in I Acts. Luke has been thought by many scholars to imitate deliberately the translation-idiom of the Greek Old Testament, especially in portions of his work where the relation to the scenes and ideas of Jewish holy writ was especially close. But in II Acts we see absolutely nothing of the sort. Even in 22, 1–21, where Paul is represented as addressing the Jews in Jerusalem " in the Hebrew language " (21, 40; 22, 2), at a time when he especially wished to show himself a Hebrew of the Hebrews, we find no Semitisms, no Biblical language, no allusion to the Scriptures.

The passage 26, 16–18 is highly interesting as showing how our author wrote under circumstances almost uniquely fitted to make him recall the words and phrases of the Old Testament. He is here composing, with entire freedom,[1] the charge given by the God of Israel to his apostle to the Gentiles on the occasion of his calling him to the great work. The writer's conception of the God whose words to Paul are here given is of course derived from the Jewish Scriptures, and the language in which the words were spoken (as we should know even if we were not expressly told in verse 14) is thought of as " Hebrew."[2] Since the Christian apostles were in a

---

[1] This appears from comparison of the parallel passages, and was to be expected from the literary habit mentioned above, the writer being quite free to adorn his narrative *ad libitum* with such material as this.

[2] Presumably Hebrew rather than Aramaic, though τῇ Ἑβραΐδι διαλέκτῳ might mean either.

true sense the successors of the Hebrew prophets, and since, too, this whole passage forms part of the address to Agrippa, who 'believed in the prophets' (vs. 27),[1] it is altogether natural that some words reminiscent of the great seers of Israel should be included in the divine announcement to Paul. It is not, I think, an over-acute vision that sees a conscious echo of Ezek. 2, 1 (call of Ezekiel) in στῆθι ἐπὶ τοὺς πόδας σου, and of Jer. 1, 7 f. (call of Jeremiah) in ἐξαιρούμενός σε . . . εἰς οὓς ἐγὼ ἀποστέλλω σε; though the phrases are very ordinary, and certainly no formal quotation is intended. It may be accidental that the only other trace of Old Testament phraseology in the whole passage is reminiscent of Isaiah, ἀνοῖξαι ὀφθαλμούς and ἀπὸ σκότους εἰς φῶς sounding more like Is. 42, 7, 16 than like any other passages in which this oft-recurring idea is expressed. But the absence here of Old Testament quotations or phrases, other than the uncertain instances just mentioned, is remarkable. The language used is well suited to its purpose, it is needless to say, and makes distinctly the impression of being the language of holy writ; there is an approach to that balancing of clauses and correspondence of phrases which is universal in the loftier passages of Semitic literature, whether Hebrew or Aramaic, poetry or prose. No one, even in modern times, who had ever read the Old Testament could write in any other way, in such a context as this. But the contrast with such passages as Luke 1, 14–17; 31–33; 35–37; 2, 9–14 (to say nothing of the *poems* in these chapters) is perfectly clear: in the Gospel the clauses are all reducible to the Hebrew line of three metrical accents, and the idioms are those of translation-Greek; here in Acts neither of these two things is true. Luke begins with a *Greek* proverb (vs. 14), proceeds with a construction (ὧν τε εἶδές με ὧν τε ὀφθήσομαί σοι, vs. 16) which is perfectly comprehensible in Greek, but absolutely inconceivable as a translation from Aramaic or Hebrew; and in the verses which follow, in which he approaches the Old Testament diction more nearly, there is nothing resembling a Semitism; indeed, the πίστει without a preposition (vs. 18) would be most unlikely as a translation in such a place as this. Yet this is the

---

[1] That vss. 24–29 give a substantially accurate account of the course of events on that occasion, I have no doubt.

writer who has been supposed by some scholars to attach a peculiar sanctity to the jargon of the Septuagint!

When the formal citations of Old Testament scripture in Acts are examined, the contrast between the two halves of the book, in the amount of such citation, is really startling. In the smaller edition of Westcott and Hort, I Acts extends over thirty-eight pages, II Acts has thirty-two. The former half is very liberally supplied with quotations; the editors have printed in uncial type and identified in their index ninety-four such (but many of these, I think, are too uncertain to be allowed); Nestle's text recognizes eighty-three. More than half of them occur in the speech of Stephen in chapter 7, but as they are there by the choice of the writer, they of course deserve to be counted with the rest. In II Acts, the Old Testament is quoted only *four times*! The passages are 17, 31 (Ps. 9, 8, or 96, 13, or 98, 9), 22, 5 (Ex. 22, 28), 25, 16 (Ezek. 2, 1 ?), and 28, 26 f. (Is. 6, 9 f.). The first of these is merely a widely current phrase; the second is probably a true report of Paul's own words, and therefore not to be counted here; the third is doubtful, because it is almost made necessary by the context. In the fourth alone do we have a formal citation; this is therefore the *only* passage in the thirteen chapters composed by Luke himself in which he expressly refers to the Hebrew scriptures. When Paul delivers an address to Jews, in this part of the book (22, 1–21; 26, 2–29) he neither appeals to the sacred volume nor employs its words in any way.[1] Contrast with this the fact that his speeches to the Jews in chapter 13 contain *eleven* Old Testament quotations! It seems plain that the reason for this great difference must lie in Luke's early training. Probably most of the Jewish and Christian writers on religious themes, in his day, were men " full of " the Old Testament, trained from early youth in the knowledge of the holy scriptures, Hebrew or Greek. Luke was not one of these. His interest in the sacred writings seems to have been a comparatively late acquisition, and their words and phrases did not come readily to his pen. He seems to have been singularly free from any personal interest in theological

---

[1] I leave 28, 26 f. out of account here, since it is not represented as part of an address, but as a parting shot delivered by Paul as the Jews were leaving after his argument with them. It is also Luke's own parting shot!

matters, and apparently had no considerable aptitude for studies in that field. This may serve to explain why we gain from Acts not the slightest conception of the great battles on behalf of Christian doctrine which Paul was fighting, with himself and with others, during all the latter part of his life. It may be doubted whether Luke had any clear understanding of the nature of these controversies. His own interests were mainly practical and humanitarian, and " the Scriptures " did not mean to him what the phrase meant to Paul and to most of his associates.

In I Acts, the treatment of Old Testament quotations by the translator is precisely the same as that which we can observe in the Third Gospel. As we have seen, Luke was Hellenist enough to give, on principle, every quotation from the Old Testament in the form in which it had stood for centuries in the Greek Bible and was familiar to those for whom he wrote.

### § 2. The Homogeneity of the Aramaic Document

In regard to the Aramaic document underlying 1, 1–15, 35, this much can be said at the outset, that in its Greek dress it gives no obvious evidence of composition. Of course every document of the nature of this one is " composite " in the sense that it is put together out of materials collected from various sources. Some of the materials used by the writer of this history may possibly have been written records (letters, memoranda, or popular narrative), and in that case we should expect them to be reproduced with little change. It is altogether probable, however, that the *main* source from which our author obtained his information of all these events was *hearsay*; and that he composed his narrative with the freedom which was customary, and in perfect good faith. Even if large sections were written entirely in his own words, on the basis of his own personal knowledge, they were at least the product of various occasions, moods, and influences. To demand perfect consistency would be unreasonable, and even a considerable measure of self-contradiction is altogether human. If the fact of translation is granted, it is not likely that any convincing theory of composition will ever be put forth.

As the Aramaic history lay before its translator, it included all that we now have in I Acts, from the first chapter to the latter part of the fifteenth. This is made certain by the uniformity in language and treatment. More than this, its beginning extended back into the first verse of the first chapter, as I shall endeavor to show.

The manner in which the book opens is sufficiently remarkable. *There is no introductory paragraph*, although we are led to expect one. Luke enters upon a prefatory sentence addressed to Theophilus, but the sentence is never finished. Of a sudden we find that it is no longer Luke that is speaking, but his source. How or where the transition is effected, there is no plain indication, yet the fact is certain. It is not merely that the μέν of vs. 1 has no corresponding δέ, nor even the inconsequence of referring to a "former" λόγος without proceeding to some mention, however brief, of the present sequel; more significant than these things is the material evidence, even before the first pause in the sentence is reached, that another than Luke is telling the story. The "forty days" of vs. 3 is quite incongruous with Luke 24, as many have observed;[1] Preuschen, *Komm.*, Wellhausen, *Analyse*, and others would reject the verse as an interpolation. The words in vs. 4: "the promise . . . *which ye have heard from me*" could never have been written by the compiler of the Third Gospel, for he knew, better than any other, that the promise here quoted was spoken by John the Baptist, not by Jesus. See the note on 11, 16, above. He softens the contradiction—but by no means removes it — by inserting his own τοῦ πατρός (Luke 24, 49). Again, even in vs. 2 there is evidence of translation, as has already been shown, similar to the indications found in the immediately succeeding parts of the chapter. The fact deserves to be

---

[1] It is not at all likely that Luke would "adopt another tradition" of the ascension and the interval immediately preceding on oral authority, after he had finished his Gospel. It is not probable that there was any considerable interval between the completion of the Gospel and that of Acts; even if there were, he had already tested and chosen his authorities. An *oral* authority, previously overlooked by him, would certainly not have been allowed to supplant completely his former account. We know that he is using a *written* source in this narrative of the beginning of the Jerusalem church; and the only reasonable conclusion we can reach is this, that his source extends back into these first verses — especially as the linguistic evidence shows the same thing.

strongly emphasized, that *there is no point after vs. 1a at which it could reasonably be claimed that Luke begins to make direct use of his document of the Jerusalem church.* Verses 15–26 are the immediate and homogeneous continuation of 6–14, and these verses in turn have an equally close literary and material connection with 4 f. But vs. 4 also presupposes just what we have in 1b–3!

The conclusion, satisfying all the evidence, is this, that Luke's proceeding here is exactly like that which we can observe in his Gospel, as well as in his subsequent use of this same document: he gives his sources the word, adding just as little as possible.[1] We may conjecture that the original beginning of the Jerusalem document was as follows: בָּתַר כָּל אִלֵּין דִּי שָׁרִי יֵשׁוּעַ לְמֶעְבַּד וּלְאַלָּפָה עַד יוֹמָא דִּי פַּקֵּד שְׁלִיחַיָּא דִּי נְבָא בְּרוּחָא דִּי קוּדְשָׁא וְאִסְתַּלַּק ·,· דִּי חַוִּי נַפְשֵׁהּ לְהוֹן כְּדִי חַי מִן בָּתַר חֲשָׁשֵׁהּ בְּאָתִין שַׂגִּיאִין כְּדִי יוֹמִין אַרְבְּעִין מִתְחֲזֵא הוּא לְהוֹן וְאָמַר הֲוָה עַל מַלְכוּתָא דִּי אֱלָהָא ·,· וּכְדִי מִתְמַלַּח הוּא עַמְּהוֹן פַּקֵּד אִנּוּן וכ׳ "After all that Jesus did and taught, up to the day when he gave commandment to the apostles, whom he had chosen by the Holy Spirit, and was taken up (to whom he also showed himself alive, with many proofs, after his passion, appearing to them during forty days and speaking the things concerning the kingdom of God): while eating in company with them, he charged them," etc. This is an eminently suitable beginning of such a church-history as the one before us; it is hard to imagine a better. It contains, moreover, just those things which are presupposed in the following narrative. If we suppose the document to have begun in these words, we have at once the explanation of Luke's procedure, which is worthy of him in its simplicity and self-restraint. He merely substituted περί, "*concerning,*" for the בָּתַר, "after," of his source, which he left otherwise untouched, and then prefixed his Τὸν μὲν πρῶτον λόγον ἐποιησάμην, ὦ Θεόφιλε. It is to be observed that the main clause, in the Aramaic original, began with vs. 4: " eating in company with them *he charged them,*" etc.

---

[1] See, for instance, in the opening chapters of his Gospel how, after a single sentence giving the briefest possible introduction to his great task, he proceeds at once with a word-for-word rendering of a Hebrew document, to which he seems to contribute no comment nor supplement of any sort. See also his treatment of the Lord's Prayer (*Aram. Gospels*, p. 309 ff.).

The " and " at the beginning of this clause is redundant in the Aramaic, as is usual in such cases, especially when the clause is introduced by בְּדִי. Of course Luke renders the conjunction.[1]

The reasons often urged in recent years for considering the early chapters of the book as composite, the work of an editor who combined written sources, I am unable to regard as valid, though I have read the arguments of Harnack and others with some diligence. Supposed differences in the theological background of different chapters are likely to be purely imaginary; our knowledge of the conditions of the time is far too meager to make such reasoning safe. In more than one place, so much general resemblance has been observed between the accounts of two successive events, or series of events, that the hypothesis of originally duplicate narratives of the same occurrences has suggested itself to some. Thus Harnack, *Apostelgeschichte*, 142–145, would make 2, 1–47 and 5, 17–42 a separate account running parallel to 3, 1–5, 16. But the repetitions, recurring situations, and similarity of treatment could not have been avoided under the circumstances. Chapter 2 tells of the gift of tongues, the resulting speech of Peter, and the effect in Jerusalem; chapter 3 f., of the first miracle of healing — with its unanswerable argument, the resulting speech of Peter, and the effect, especially on the Jewish authorities. The narrative of these two occurrences must inevitably seem to return upon itself to some extent, since the general situation, the chief actors, and the exciting incident (a miracle) were necessarily the same in both cases. But the two events are essentially different from each other, and each is highly significant in its own way. The second is the natural sequel to the first, and I do not see how it is possible to deny that there is progress in the narrative from one to the other. Wendt, *Komm.*, 98 (on 2, 43–47) writes: " In V. 43 ist von vielen Wundertaten der App. und dem furchterregenden

---

[1] What has so often been said in regard to the necessity of a formal " literary " introduction to this second treatise of Luke falls to the ground as soon as the translation is recognized. The author was not only under no stylistic necessity whatever, but the strict interpretation of his task moved him to put himself in the background as soon and as far as possible. Everything needful in the way of introduction to the work is done in the words which we actually have before us.

Eindrucke derselben[1] die Rede, während doch in K. 3 u. 4 der Bericht über die Lahmenheilung und die anschliessenden Verhandlungen so ausgeführt wird, als sei dies das erste (4, 16) offenkundige Wunder der Jünger gewesen, die man bisher noch nicht als im Namen Jesu wirkend gekannt hätte (vgl. zu 4, 7)." But is not a writing — even an ancient writing — entitled to the interpretation which makes it self-consistent rather than self-contradictory? It is only by a forced exegesis of the passages in question that these discrepancies can be created; the text itself does not readily suggest them, and they have been overlooked by the vast majority of commentators. The same thing is true, so far as I have observed, of all the other discrepancies and contradictions which have recently been pointed out in I Acts: they are such as are easily found by those who are in search of them, but could hardly seem convincing to the reader who is equally inclined to regard the whole account as the work of a single author.

Some scholars have regarded chapters 13 and 14 as belonging to a source different from that of the preceding chapters. The language of both, however, is distinctly translation-Greek, see the notes above, and the narrative which they contain is essential to the plan and purpose of the Aramaic history of the early church, as I hope to show presently. Many commentators have been impressed by the resemblance, in both substance and form, between the speech of the apostles at Lystra (14, 15-17) and the address of Paul at Athens (17, 22-31). Wendt, *Komm.*, 254 (cf. 220), pronounces the Lystra speech an imitation (Nachbildung) of the other; and the opinion is often expressed that the same writer must have composed both. The striking resemblances are due mainly, however, to the similarity of situation in the two passages. In each case Paul is represented as addressing highly cultivated pagans by whom he has been well received and whom he hopes to impress favorably, and the starting point of each of the two speeches happens to be furnished him by the religious beliefs of these peoples: in the one case, the attempted

---

[1] Since this item is derived (see Wendt's following note) from a reading which most editors and commentators have regarded as manifestly inferior (Preuschen does not even mention it), we may safely discount the argument obtained from it here.

sacrifice; in the other, the altar to the "unknown god." Also, as we have seen, there are certain fundamental ideas which could hardly be absent in any typical missionary address to pagans. It seems probable, however, that II Acts was not written until after I Acts had been translated into Greek, and in that case it would have been very natural for Luke to bring into the speech at Athens some unconscious reminiscence of that at Lystra. *Linguistically*, be it noted, the two speeches are strongly contrasted. In 14, 15 ff. the Greek is fashioned upon its Semitic original. Εὐαγγελιζόμενοι renders בסר, which means not only "bring good tidings" (the customary rendering) but also simply "exhort." Ματαίων presumably represents טָעְוָתָא (cf. Deut. 32, 21; Jer. 8, 19, etc.), literally "errors," a somewhat more conciliatory word than the Greek. Ἐπὶ θεὸν ζῶντα (without the article!) renders exactly the Aramaic equivalent (אֱלָהּ חַי, Ps. 42, 3; אֱלָהּ קַיָּם, Jos. 3, 10) of the standing Hebrew phrase אֵל חַי, "*the* living God," Jos. 3, 10; Hos. 2, 1; Ps. 42, 3; 84, 3; 2 Kings 19, 4, 16, etc. The clause from the Old Testament is a real citation, and not merely a remote parallel, as in 17, 24. And finally, there is the mistranslation of מכל, see the note on the passage. In 17, 22 ff., on the contrary, everything is native Greek. The word δεισιδαιμονεστέρους, for example, could not be a translation, nor is there any Semitic word which could naturally have been rendered by ἀγνώστῳ (θεῷ). Such phrases as ζωὴν καὶ πνοὴν and πάντας πανταχοῦ would not be found in chapters 1–15. And finally, there is the *Greek* quotation in vs. 28. The true relation of the two speeches is thus quite evident.

There is nothing in the order of the chapters 12–15, so far as I can see, that gives ground for any suspicion of editorial composition or disarrangement, and the order of events seems to me entirely logical and probable. It is plain to see why the change from "Saul" to "Paul" was made in chapter 13. The Aramaic document very probably kept the name שָׁאוּל throughout. But to have preserved it thus in the Greek translation, reserving the change until 15, 36 ff., would have been disturbing on more than one account. There was no evident reason why the change of name should be made at the point where Luke's own narrative began. The effect would certainly also have been to make apparent the fact of composition. But the main consideration was certainly this, that the logical place for introducing the new name was the point where the "Apostle to the Gentiles" began the great foreign labors which were his chief glory and by reason of which the apostles held their council in Jerusalem. To the Jews and Christians of Palestine he was still "Saul of Tarsus," but the name by which he was known all through the Greek-speaking world was *Paul*. Naturally, therefore, the place to begin the use of the latter name was the account of his first great missionary journey.

There is good reason to believe that in 15, 35 we have the original conclusion of Luke's Aramaic source. This is the natural place for the Judean document to come to an end, for the story of the first distinct period of the Christian church in Jerusalem has been written. Peter has initiated the work among the Gentiles. Paul and Barnabas have gained their first great successes as foreign missionaries. The Mother Church has sent out its circular letter, voicing its own supreme authority and at the same time making Gentile Christianity permanently free from the regulations of Judaism. The verses 15, 30–35 are admirably suited to bring the book to a close. The Gentiles, represented by the foremost Gentile Christian city, Antioch, receive their charter of freedom with joy; Judas and Silas return to Jerusalem; Paul and Barnabas remain in Antioch, "teaching and preaching, with many others, the word of the Lord."

The point of view and purpose of the whole document may be described in this way. A man of Judea, presumably of Jerusalem, undertook to set forth the main facts touching the growth of the Christian church from the little band of Jews left behind by Jesus to the large and rapidly growing body, chiefly Gentile, whose branches were in all parts of the world. He was a man of catholic spirit and excellent literary ability. He wrote in Aramaic, and with great loyalty to the Holy City and the Twelve Apostles, and yet at the same time with genuine enthusiasm for the mission to the Gentiles and its foremost representatives, especially Paul. His chief interest was in *the universal mission* of Christianity (1, 8; 2, 5 ff.; 3, 25; 7, 48–53; 10, 1–11, 18; 11, 21; 13, 46 ff.; 15, etc.). He was secondarily interested to show — what the far-seeing among the Jewish Christians of his time must generally have acknowledged — that although the new faith was first developed, of necessity, among the Jews, yet being rejected by the main body of them it passed out of their hands. From the very beginning of his account, he had in mind as its central feature the wonderful transition from Jewish sect to world-religion. From the outset he purposed to show how Antioch became the first great Gentile center of Christianity; his pride in Antioch was of course hardly equal to his pride in Jerusalem, but was very real nevertheless. It is a skillful arrangement of his material by which he makes it all lead up, in successive steps, to the first great triumphs of the new faith on foreign soil, and to the true climax in chapter 15. It may be added, that there is nothing in Acts 1–15 which seems out of harmony with this general purpose. There are unquestionably strong reasons for concluding that Luke has preserved for us, practically intact, the whole of the Aramaic narrative which had come into his hands; and perhaps equally cogent reasons for believing that this document had not been pieced together from fragmentary written sources, but rather composed entire by a single Judean narrator.

From their different points of view Luke and the Judean narrator were aiming to set forth precisely the same thing. Their main premises and chief arguments were practically identical, for the purposes of such a history as this, and it was therefore an easy matter for the Hellenist to continue from the point where the Jewish convert had left off. Their joint work is truly typical of what was taking place at that time on so great a scale.

### § 3. The Probable Date of Acts

The foregoing investigation has made it possible, through the demonstration of the Aramaic Document and its translation by the same writer who composed its sequel, to establish a degree of probability never before attainable in regard to the authorship and composition of the book; and it will readily be seen that the question of dates, for Acts and the Third Gospel, is also considerably simplified.

Acts 15, 36–28, 31 was written by a contemporary and companion of Paul.[1] The writer seems to have met the apostle first at Troas, in the year 50,[2] and to have accompanied his party to Philippi. On the return of Paul to the latter city, in the year 58 or 59, Luke again joined the apostle and his companions, and went with them on their journey to Jerusalem. From this time on, he seems to have regarded himself as one of Paul's adherents; and after the two years' imprisonment of the latter at Caesarea (59–61) he accompanied him on the journey to Rome, arriving in 62.

Evidence that the account was written not long after the events described is also to be found in the occasional presence in the narrative of purely incidental details of personal interest, such as might naturally be inserted by one to whom the occurrences were still fresh in mind, and who was writing for men to whom the persons and incidents mentioned were also well known. Such details are the introduction of Mnason in 21, 16; the mention of the "sign of the Dioscuri" in 28, 11; the allusions to Jason (as a well-known personage) in 17, 5–9, and to Alexander in 19, 33. Hence also probably the ἀμφοτέρων and ἐκ τοῦ οἴκου ἐκείνου, 19, 16, in the story of the sons of the Jew Sceva[3] — the anecdote being a familiar one. Other examples will occur to readers of the book. On the other hand, it must be said that not even the story of the journey to Rome gives the impression of a record made at the very time of the occurrences described. It does not sound at all like a "journal" or "travel-diary," but rather like subsequent recollection aided by the recollection of others.

Nothing can be learned with certainty from the manner in which the book comes to an end. This much, however, may be said to be highly *probable*: that 28, 31 formed the original and intended close of the book; and that this verse was written *after* Paul had been transferred from his "hired dwelling" to a veritable prison, and *before* Luke had received news of his death. Paul had many friends

---

[1] There seems to be no good reason why the church tradition, that the writer was Luke, should not be retained, as certainly possible and perhaps well founded.

[2] I follow the chronology adopted by Wendt, *Komm.*, p. 64.

[3] I can hardly believe that the word ἀρχιερέως stood in the original text.

and followers in Rome, and the fact of his death — or of his release from prison — would almost certainly have become known within a short time. The year 64, then, may be regarded as the most probable date of the writing of chapters 16–28. This whole second half of the book could easily have been written at Rome within a few weeks' time, Luke having there the aid of men (such as Aristarchus, and perhaps Timothy) who had accompanied Paul in the journeys in which he himself did not participate. This hypothesis at least agrees with all the known facts.

Since II Acts was written as the sequel of I Acts, it is altogether reasonable to suppose that the idea of writing this history was first suggested to Luke when the Aramaic Document came into his hands. We have no reason to suppose, but very good reasons against supposing, that he had in mind such a history while he was making his journeys in company with Paul. If the plan of writing it had already occurred to him, we may be sure that he would have made notes of a very different character from the incidental, loosely connected, and often unimportant reminiscences which now occupy so large a part of the work. We may conjecture that the Document came into his hands either when Paul was in prison at Caesarea, during which time (two years) Luke was very likely in Palestine, or — even more probably — after his arrival in Rome in the year 62.[1] Judging from the very cautious manner in which he handled the Document, not venturing to alter it or omit from it, even when he believed it to be wrong (see above), it would seem fairly certain that he did not know who its author was, and had no means of finding out. He could hardly have studied it *in Palestine*, moreover, without becoming aware of the true meaning of certain passages which must have perplexed him, such as 11, 27–30, and others, mentioned above, in which the unfamiliar Palestinian idiom made trouble for him. The supposition that he found the Document in Rome is the one which best suits the facts before us. The Document was written in Palestine after the Council of the Apostles at Jerusalem in the year 49, prob-

---

[1] An alternative amounting to the same thing is the supposition that he secured the Document before leaving Palestine, but did not decide to make this use of it until after his arrival in Rome.

ably very soon after that event and under the inspiration of the wonderful beginning of the work among the Gentiles. It is a very significant fact that its author *did not know* (see 15, 32 f.) *that Silas had started on a new missionary journey in company with Paul.* A man of his interests and information could not have remained for many months in ignorance of this most important turn of events. We are accordingly enabled to date the Document with unusual precision; it must have been composed late in the year 49, or early in the year 50.

In relation to the Third Gospel, the Book of Acts was plainly *an afterthought.* When Luke wrote his brief prologue to the former treatise, he certainly did not have in mind the continuation which included his own personal experiences.[1] On the other hand, in the latter treatise, the extreme brevity of the address to Theophilus, without explanation or further remark, makes the conclusion practically certain (as scholars have generally agreed) that the interval between the two writings was a short one. Now the all-important feature of Luke's own labors in compiling his Gospel history (see my *Translations made from the Original Aramaic Gospels,* pp. 288–297) was the searching out and employing of "authentic" documents, that is, of *Palestinian sources* in their original Semitic form. The collection of such material could only be made in Palestine, and would necessarily occupy considerable time. It is certainly a striking coincidence, that a few years before the date which has seemed most probable for the composition of Acts, Luke should have made an extended stay in Palestine. It is a conjecture which is more than merely plausible, that during the two years (24, 27) of Paul's imprisonment at Caesarea Luke was collecting, examining, and translating the materials for his Gospel. We may then venture the conclusion, that the Third Gospel was written before the year 61, probably in the year 60.

[1] The latter treatise, moreover, could not have been described in the same terms as the former. In the Gospel, Luke did indeed "trace the course of all things accurately from the first," with laborious comparison and criticism of authorities and incorporation of new Palestinian material. The Book of Acts, on the contrary, was not a work of research, nor even of any considerable labor. It was merely the translation of a single document — a lucky find — supplemented by a very brief outline of Paul's missionary labors, enlivened by miscellaneous personal reminiscences.

To the hypothesis of such an early date for the Lukan writings the advocates of a later dating have been wont to oppose two objections which, if their validity could be established, would be truly fatal. These are, first, the supposed evidence in Luke 21, 20–24 of a date subsequent to the destruction of Jerusalem; and second, the alleged dependence of Acts on Josephus.

Those who argue from the passage in the Gospel point to the divergences from the parallel in Mark (13, 14–20). Thus Wendt, *Komm.*, 46 note, insists that since Luke predicts the siege and destruction of Jerusalem, and also speaks of a period after the catastrophe during which the Gentiles will triumph for a time (the καιροὶ ἐθνῶν), and *since these things are not in Mark*, therefore the Third Gospel must have been written after the year 70. Similarly Wellhausen, *Evangelium Lucae*, 117 f., basing his whole argument on the assumption that the only sources of Luke 21, 20–24 were the passage in Mark and the actual progress of events. But may not the author of the later passage also be supposed to have known the Old Testament scriptures? To be sure, it must be said that on the sole basis of Mark the prediction would have been easy enough. When he speaks of ἐρήμωσις, foretells the frantic flight of the citizens to the mountains, and adds, that there will be then " such distress as there has not been since the creation of the world, and never shall be," no one could possibly doubt that the capture of the city, and its ἐρήμωσις, were foretold. The language in Luke is very cautious. Jerusalem had been " *compassed with armies* " and captured by these Roman invaders more than once already; must not the great final catastrophe be incomparably more terrible than anything preceding, even surpassing the slaughter and captivity in the days of Nebuchadrezzar? So Mark had said. But this is not all. Verse 22 in Luke must not be overlooked: these calamities are to come " so that all things which are written may be fulfilled." This is a very significant addition, and it is not easy to understand how it can have been left out of account by some of those who have compared the three Gospels at this important point. The predictions in the Old Testament were certainly explicit enough. The end of the present age is described in Zech. 14, 1 ff.: " A day of Yahwè cometh, when thy spoil shall be divided in the midst of thee. For I will gather all nations against Jerusalem to battle; and *the city shall be taken*, and the houses rifled, and the women ravished; and *half the city shall go forth into captivity.*" This last phrase indicates plainly enough the interval between the slaughter and devastation and the final triumph of Yahwè and his people, described in verses 3 ff. So also Daniel had prophesied. The last and most terrible beast " shall wear out the saints of the Most High " (7, 25), " and they shall be given into his hand for a time and times (καιρῶν) and half a time." Dan. 8, 13 had declared that at the time of the פֶּשַׁע שֹׁמֵם, ἁμαρτία ἐρημώσεως (the very thing spoken of by Mark), the sanctuary should be *trampled under foot*, Lk., πατουμένη ὑπὸ ἐθνῶν. And again, in Dan. 12, 1, 7, the prophet foretold the time that must elapse *between* the ἐρήμωσις, when " there shall be a time of trouble such as never was since there was a nation even to that same time " (vs. 1; Mark 13, 19), and the day of final triumph when Michael shall stand forth and deliver the holy people. The interval will be (vs. 7) "a time, times (καιρούς), and a half," until " they have made an end of breaking in pieces the power of the holy people "; that is, to the end of the καιροὶ ἐθνῶν. It appears, then, that *every particle* of Luke's prediction not provided by Mark was furnished by familiar and oft-quoted Old Testament passages. It is therefore obviously not permissible to call Luke 21, 20–24 a *vaticinium ex eventu*, and it cannot be cited as throwing light on the date of the Gospel.

The argument for the dependence of the Lukan writings on Josephus has been set forth exhaustively by Krenkel, *Josephus und Lukas*. After examining his material, I agree with those scholars who find only two of his " correspondences " worthy of serious attention; namely, the Theudas-Judas passage, Acts 5, 36 f., cf. Jos., *Antt.*, xx, 5, 1 f.; and the " Lysanias tetrarch of Abilene " in Luke 3, 1, cf. *Antt.*, xx, 7, 1. On these two instances of agreement see Schmiedel, *Encyclopaedia Biblica*, articles " Judas of Galilee," " Lysanias," and " Theudas," and Burkitt, *The Gospel History and its Transmission*, 105–110, both of whom accept Krenkel's conclusion; also Wendt, *Komm.*, 42 ff., who finds cogent evidence only in the Theudas-Judas passage.

Josephus generally used written sources, and is following such a source in *Antt.* xx, 5, 1 f.; see Hölscher, *Quellen des Josephus*, 69 f. In this written authority, Theudas "the prophet" and his band were described, under the procuratorship of Cuspius Fadus. Then followed the account of his successor, Tiberius Alexander (xx, 5, 2). The chapter telling of his administration seems to have contained, in the source: (1) a brief account of the man himself, and of the family to which he belonged; (2) some account of the famine of that time (Jos. had already described this, xx, 2, 5, in another connection); (3) the story of the execution, by crucifixion, of James and Simon, the two sons of "Judas of Galilee." In telling their story, the narrator must of necessity have told something about the revolt led by Judas (Jos. remarks that he himself has told this already, namely in xvii, 10, 5). The revolt was a thing of very slight importance, hardly worthy of mention; but the execution of *the two sons* by crucifixion — imagine the horror it must have aroused in Judea! — seems to have been the most striking event of the procuratorship of Tiberius Alexander. Any history dealing with this period would have been pretty certain to mention Theudas and Judas at this point, and in this order, although the revolt under Judas really happened much earlier. From some history of the kind, in which the facts were not clearly stated, the author of Luke's Aramaic source obtained his wrong impression of the order of events. He could not easily have obtained it from the Antiquities, for the correct statement is given there very plainly and briefly; and that this was *not* his source, is shown by the number, "four hundred," in Acts 5, 36. Josephus exaggerates, as usual, with his τὸν πλεῖστον ὄχλον. The writer in Acts, who is not at all inclined toward understatement, certainly did not get his number, 400, *nor his impression of the size of the disturbance*, from the *Antiquities*, but from an older account.

Luke's statement in his Gospel, 3, 1, that "in the fifteenth year of the reign of Tiberius Caesar," etc., Lysanias was tetrarch of Abilene, is a mistake, since the tetrarch of that name was executed by Mark Antony in the year 36 B.C. Josephus, *Antt.* xx, 7, 1, in telling of the redistribution of Palestinian provinces by Claudius in the twelfth year of his reign, says that Agrippa received the tetrarchy of Philip, and Batanea, also Trachonitis with Abila, "which last had been the tetrarchy of Lysanias." Does not this show dependence of Luke on Josephus?

We know that long after the death of Lysanias the tetrarchy of Abila continued to be called by his name. See for example Josephus, *Bell. Jud.*, ii, 11, 5 (which is the parallel to *Antt.*, xx, 7, 1): ἑτέραν βασιλείαν τὴν Λυσανίου καλουμένην. If the province was "so-called," it is hardly necessary to argue further; but a few more facts may be noted. The *Antt.* passage is entirely independent of that in the *Wars*, belonging to a different context, and *from a different source* — the same source, according to Hölscher, *op. cit.*, as that from which the Theudas-Judas passage was derived. Again, we read in *Antt.*, xix, 5, 1: Ἄβιλαν δὲ τὴν Λυσανίου . . . προσετίθει κ.τ.ἑ.; and *Antt.*, xviii, 6, 10 tells how Agrippa was given the Abilene, and calls it simply τὴν Λυσανίου τετραρχίαν. Hölscher, 64 f., pronounces the source here different from either of the others above referred to. There is no need, then, to ask where Luke got his "Tetrarchy of Lysanias." He might have found it in any source he laid his hand on, since it was the ordinary way of speaking of the district of Abila; which, it may be added, would be pretty certain to appear by the side of Trachonitis in any account of the distribution of these provinces. It is very natural that Luke should have been misled.

The general conclusion may therefore be ventured, that in the facts now known to us there is nothing opposed to the results reached above in regard to the composition and dating of Acts.

www.ingramcontent.com/pod-product-compliance
Lightning Source LLC
Chambersburg PA
CBHW051706090426
42736CB00013B/2560